AN EDWARDIAN CHI
THE MAKING OF A NAT

JONATHAN HUTCHINSON
OF SELBY

MASSEY SIR JONATHAN HENRY MARK DEBORAH EDWARD ALFRED CHARLES FRANCIS ELIZABETH ARTHUR
         1828-1913   m.   m. MARY GRAHAM   m. ALICE MORLEY   m.   m.   m.   m. GEORGE WOODS
         OF LONDON AND
         HASLEMERE
         m. JANE WEST

                                    KATHLEEN   GERTRUDE OSWALD   EVELYN   ELIZABETH KATHLEEN   HILDA
                                    m. A. SAXBY HURST (TRUDA)   (EFFIE)   (ELLA)   (KITTY)
                                                                             m. EDWARD ROSHER   1875-1960

                                    ALEXANDER MURIEL   EVELYN ELIZABETH KATHLEEN
                                                                                     (FREDERICK
                                                                                      FRANCIS)

ELIZABETH JONATHAN ETHEL PROCTER LLEWELLYN ROGER HERBERT URSULA AGNES BERNARD
(ELSIE)   m.   m.   1868-1957
m.   ALLEN CHANDLER   ELEANOR TERRY m. 'ELLA' WOODS
THOS: NEWMAN

           ALLEN KATHERINE PRUNELLA   ELSIE MARJORIE NORAH JUDITH AUDREY JONATHAN
           (REX)   m.   m.   m.   m.   m.   m.   m.
                  m. JOAN COVENTRY

GEORGE HERBERT JONATHAN CHRISTOPHER MARGARET HUGH MARY RACHEL LAURENCE
1896-   (BERTEL) (JAN)   1901-   1904-   1907- 1909- 1913-   1917-
m.   1898-1918 1900-1972 m.   m.   m.   m.   m.
                  m.

"OUR LOT"

AN EDWARDIAN CHILDHOOD
THE MAKING OF A NATURALIST

Margaret Hutchinson

Author of
Children as Naturalists

An Edwardian Childhood – the Making of a Naturalist
First published 1981 (second edition 1983)
as *A Childhood in Edwardian Sussex*
by Saiga Publishing Co. Ltd

This edition published with additions 2003

Typeset and published by John Owen Smith
19 Kay Crescent, Headley Down, Hampshire GU35 8AH
Tel: 01428 712892 – Fax: 08700 516554
E-mail: wordsmith@johnowensmith.co.uk

ISBN 1-873855-47-8

Text printed and bound by Antony Rowe Ltd, Eastbourne

DEDICATION

For my sixteen Nephews and Nieces

The legend of "*The Good Old Days lives on*"

FROM THE PUBLISHER

In preparing this edition of Margaret Hutchinson's *Edwardian Childhood* to celebrate the centenary of her birth (1904), we have taken the opportunity to add further illustrations and an extra chapter which was found recently among her papers. It was written some time after the original book, in answer to the recurring question, 'But what happened next?'

There is also an additional Postscript written by Penny Hollow who knew the author well.

ACKNOWLEDGEMENTS

The encouragement and assistance of Penny Hollow and others at Haslemere Museum in the preparation of this edition is gratefully acknowledged. Robert Hutchinson, Margaret Hutchinson's nephew, and Elizabeth Dick, her niece, kindly gave permission for us to republish the original text and ED supplied the manuscript of 'Recollections of Kingsley Green'.

Most illustrations included in this book come either from the Hutchinson family or from the archives of Haslemere Museum. Photographs from both sources include many taken by Kathleen Woods ('Aunt Kitty') and Elizabeth Newman ('Aunt Elsie') between about 1889 and 1914.

Simon Futcher kindly agreed to the publication of photographs by his father, Colin Futcher.

The family tree 'Our Lot' was drawn by Margaret Hutchinson in 1981.

Photograph acknowledgements:
Haslemere Museum – pp.66, 76, 80, 85, 110, 114, 116, 118, 122, 125, 130, 138, 154, 158, 164
Keats Harding – p.133
Lane Fox, Haslemere – p.152

Chapter heading illustrations – Margaret Hutchinson

Cover:
Sketches by Margaret Hutchinson
Family photograph of children with steam engine (front cover)
Arnold Madgwick – photograph of Margaret Hutchinson (back cover)

CONTENTS

LIST OF ILLUSTRATIONS

The family at Moses Hill, 1913:
Standing *(L to R) Margaret, Jan, Bertel, Christopher*
Seated *(L to R) Herbert Hutchinson with Mary, Elizabeth H with Rachel,*
George; **Kneeling** *Hugh*

THE GUTTERING CANDLE

Delight and liberty
the simple creed of childhood
Jonathan Hutchinson

Moses Hill Farm

THE GUTTERING CANDLE

LOOKING BACK

1970 ... There was a flash of lightning and a clap of thunder. The lights flickered and went out. We were in total darkness. I groped for my torch, went to the kitchen and lit the two candles we kept ready for just such an emergency, and took one to my elderly invalid aunt who had already gone to bed. She also had a torch but I gave her the candle instead.

A little later when I went in to see if she was alright I found she had blown out the candle and left the torch on.

"You'll wear out the battery," I said, "and I can't get another tonight. We've lots of candles."

"I didn't want to waste it," she replied. "Look at all that grease dripping down. Horrible!"

"But don't you remember," I accused her laughing, "all those years and years when we lived with guttering candles? I used to chew that dripping part. Dirty little girl!"

I sat on her bed and we reminisced over the days before the magic of electricity put an end to the dirt and messiness of candles and oil lamps with which Aunt Hilda had lived far longer than I had.

The electric light came on again, suddenly, silently, with no effort on our part, but my mind had gone right back over sixty years when Mother would admonish us children as we started upstairs to bed: "Mind the candle. Hold it straight and don't spill grease on the stairs."

I enjoyed my candle. I read by it, I played with it. The grease liquefied in a little crucible of its own making at the base of the black, curved wick, till it overflowed and trickled, hardening as it went down the side of the candle. Often I would make a dent in the side of the crucible with a match, and precipitate a cascade of grease. Or I would make a pattern around the edge, creating a series of tiny cascades.

One could roll candle grease in one's fingers and make worms, or put a roll around one's teeth and pretend one had a denture like a grown-up. The wick would grow a blob on the end and dip down into the molten grease. Then one had to lift it out with a match and knock off the end.

The flickering candle cast lights and shadows about the room, particularly fascinating ones if the room had a sloping ceiling. When you carried it upstairs and along the draughty passage you had to shield the flame with one hand to prevent it going out. In my own house at least, I was never afraid of the dark, perhaps because of the flickering lights I grew up with.

Downstairs in the living-room were table lamps. Each morning the wicks had to be trimmed to get the soot off, the funnels cleaned, and the oil-wells refilled. Every now and then a new wick had to be put in. This seemed to be a tricky business for it did not always catch on the ratchet that wound it up and down.

Not infrequently the flame grew too high. Then there would be a blackened glass chimney and black soot floated about the room, getting up one's nostrils. Some people hung a hairpin on the top of the funnel believing that this prevented smoking, but I doubt if there was any truth in this.

Our grown-ups were always on the look-out for trouble with the table lamps. When we children got rampaging around the room of a winter's evening, Mother would call out "Mind the lamp!" and we would have to simmer down. There was a heavy serge table-cloth and always the fear that some sturdy toddler (there were always toddlers in our family!) would pull on this and drag the whole lot over on top of itself. But this is how we lived, and I can say now without any fear of "tempting Providence" that we never had an accident with lamps or bedside candles. Or in fact with open wood and coal fires generally well screened behind fireguards; or with the large, black kitchen range that dropped red-hot coals into the brass fender below.

MY FIRST HOME – MOSES HILL FARM

All this took place at the home I first remember that went by the quaint name of Moses Hill Farm. As a child I had a vague idea that Moses had struck a rock up on that lovely hill-top in Sussex. Later I learned its true origin, which I had better explain at once to set the scene for the first nine years of my life as a country child before the First World War changed everything.

The oldest part of the farm dated back probably to Plantagenet times, at any rate before chimneys were thought of. There was a central room going right up to the roof. A fire was made in the centre and smoke rose up and out through a hole in the top. In the process the sturdy oak beams became blackened, and though it must have been much more uncomfortable to live with than our candles and oil lamps, it helped to preserve the timbers.

The farm was originally called "Highfields," an obvious name for it stands on the crest of the hill 700 feet above sea-level. By 1539, however, a farmer of the name of John Mose was there. It is from him that the name has persisted. It is said, but on what authority I do not know, that a certain Mr Mose took his wife all the way to London to be cured of the King's Evil, Scrofula, by being touched by Charles I. The forty-five mile journey in those days must have been quite a venture, for roads were miry and highwaymen were not unknown.

Little boy (Christopher)
standing with a stick

From time to time the farmhouse was altered and extended. At one stage it belonged to the Cowdrays of Cowdray Park, Midhurst, and was used as a hunting (or was it merely shooting?) lodge. By the time our family moved into it there was a dear old Sussex couple, Mr and Mrs Tom Wheeler, living in the oldest corner, which was a self-contained cottage. The rest, part very old, part newer, was a house of two living rooms and kitchen and five or six bedrooms. It even had a bathroom with hot and cold!

We moved up to Moses Hill from Haslemere, our nearest town over two miles away, when I was a few months old, so I do not remember that. Apparently Christopher, three years my senior, had had scarlet fever and he and a governess, Miss Smith, went first to remove him from the family. I like the faded photo of the curly-headed little boy standing with a stick (all country boys brandished sticks – it is part of their boy nature) by the faggots stacked against a corner of the house. They were used to light the fires.

It must have been a strange, lonely life with only the Wheelers next door, until the main contingent joined them.

My own earliest recollections are of the various rooms, the farm buildings and, of course, the people around me. Curiously, the part of the house I remember best is upstairs. Two of my brothers slept in a bedroom in the oldest part of the house, with a steep sloping roof, a dormer window and black, black beams and rafters. There was just room to get in along one side of each bed without bumping your head on the beams. It was on brother Jan's bed that I used to sit for what seemed like hours as he brushed and combed my hair and tied it up in ribbons. He was just enjoying himself trying out different effects. I could lay it at his door that he brushed all the wave out of my hair, for early photos show me with a pretty wave, but by the age of twelve it was straight and lank like seaweed.

EARLY DAYS

It was said that, when I, the eldest girl, was born, and my four brothers were shown their first sister, one of them remarked: "But we wanted a proper sort of girl, one with hair!" I wonder if this was Jan also?

It was into this boys' bedroom one Christmas morning early that I had trotted, clutching my Christmas stocking. As we opened our stockings and cracked nuts and chewed sticky sweets in the half dark one of the boys spilt the beans about Father Christmas. "I know who it is," he said, "it's Mother and Father really."

I did not want to believe him, but gradually the penny dropped, and being a matter-of-fact sort of child I was not unduly disturbed. The main concern was to hide one's discovery from one's parents, for it was well known that as soon as one knew the facts, Father Christmas ceased to call. Already George had stopped hanging up his stocking, and I felt quite sorry for him.

There was another curious room in which another brother, generally Christopher, slept. Its oddness lay in the fact that it had a window at floor level. Aunt Kitty was an expert photographer. One day, erecting the fire-dogs and fire irons in front of the window, she took photos of several of us by "fire-light." This was, of course, before the days of flash-light photography, and the light used was strong sunlight coming through the window.

One went up two or three steps from this room into my parents' bedroom over the drawing-room, which was the newest part of the house. In a corner of this quite large room I had my little bed, under a window that looked right over the garden. Though I did not remember this until I saw this room quite recently, the big window at the other end of the room commanded a magnificent view across the end of

Blackdown and right over the weald of Sussex to the South Downs. It is interesting now to look back and realise that the things one remembers so vividly are the scenes nearer home, the places where I roamed and played. Young children are not nearly so much influenced by the grandeur of a distant view.

I am not being very chronological in my description of upstairs for I am sure that before this I must have slept in the night nursery with a nurse or "Mother's help", whichever reigned at the time, until a new arrival came to push me out.

New arrivals came three times in the nine years we were at Moses Hill. First Hugh, then Mary and lastly Rachel. Even she was not destined to remain the youngest of the family, for four years later came along what ought to have been called Benjamin, but in reality was named Laurence. Mother got a fancy for the name from reading many times over to us Louisa Alcott's *Little Women* and *Little Men*.

To return to the parents' bedroom in which I remember sleeping. Hugh, having now been pushed out of the night nursery by

Aunt Kitty photographed Christopher and Margaret by "fire-light"

Mary, was sleeping with Christopher, and each morning he would hold up a corner of his nightie so that he didn't trip on it, and tiptoe up the steps into our room for a good play with me before it was time to get dressed. It seems we always played "Christening the Baby." Being Quakers our babies were not baptised and this made the ceremony as we had seen it performed in Children's services at Fernhurst parish church all the more dramatic. So this is where Hugh's nightie became so important. It made a perfect surplice. Hugh stood solemnly beside the washstand and I stood opposite holding my baby doll.

There were two things that happened to most babies, though only one of them to ours. So it is understandable that Hugh, with as reverent a voice as his four years could manage, announced one day: "Now it is time to vaccinate the baby!" "Silly," I replied scornfully, "you mean christen." Much later when Laurence was being vaccinated we children as usual gathered round to watch. Bits of lint and sticking plaster were placed on the table. Mother held the chubby baby's arm while the doctor made the jabs – four of them. He placed the lint over them and then hunted for the plaster. Christopher, who had a bubbling sense of humour, was holding his sides in his efforts not to explode, for the plaster was stuck on the doctor's elbow.

It is with some amusement that one reflects that Hugh did in fact grow up to baptise many infants, but being a Congregationalist he did not have to wear a nightie. Despite a strong bias towards medicine in earlier generations, none of my brothers or sisters ever vaccinated anyone.

Every two or three years our dear Nurse Castle would come to stay, with a large Gladstone bag. I would be removed to another room to sleep, Mother would retire to bed, and there would be a certain hush about the house, though very pleasant because Nurse was our visitor. Then one morning we would be ushered into Mother's room to see the tiny baby lying in bed with her. I remember no feeling of jealousy, only excitement and love for this new arrival.

As Nurse came several times, however, we did begin to be suspicious and I remember Christopher drawing me aside and suggesting in a whisper, "Do you think Nurse has brought another baby?" Sometimes we asked her outright, only to be answered with her delightful chuckle and a fond caress. After all there *were* times when she visited us and no babies materialised, but then she only came for the day.

But that Gladstone bag was a bit awesome. We would glance anxiously at it. I never liked the idea of a baby in one of those, but we never had the nerve to look in, unlike some other "customers" Nurse told me of later on, whom she caught having a good hunt in it.

Nurse stayed a whole month. Mother lay in bed three weeks, reading and feeding the baby, (fascinating that we were allowed to watch), and presently (after the umbilical cord had come away) we stood around enchanted at the ceremony of bathing the baby. How gentle Nurse was, how smiling, how devoted to her work.

I only once remember feeling embarrassed and that was when I asked of the well wrapped up infant how they knew it was a girl? The grown-ups exchanged glances and I was "put off". Of course, the penny dropped as soon as I saw it being bathed, for we younger children bathed and dressed together and we knew the difference between boys and girls just like that.

I think, brought up as we were, most pennies dropped in time though we were really told nothing for a very long time.

GLIMPSE AT RELATIVES

Out in Africa at a little place called Heaney Junction on the railway line near Bulawayo five months after my arrival on earth, by whatever means we were not told, three babies, triplets were born to Mother's sister, our Aunt Effie. They caused a great stir, not only out there, but back home also.

Comments such as "may one be spared," "only the poor do such things," and, "were they born with their eyes open?" were made. This last one was made by a middle-aged spinster. Unmarried ladies were not supposed to know much about babies, unless perchance they became involved.

The triplet's aunt, Miss Ethel Rosher, had gone out to help with the new baby. Being an eminently practical soul she had read up about birth before setting out. This was indeed a good thing for in the event she found herself with the help of a neighbour delivering not one, not two, but three. She managed magnificently and, despite the gloomy forebodings back home, they not only lived but are all alive and well in this year of grace 1980. They are Betty, Fred and Frank and will come into this story several times.

They had an older sister Evelyn, who had had the stage to herself for five years. Now the whole household revolved around these squealing infants, and one's heart bleeds for poor Evelyn.

Unlike us, she had been told where babies came from. Aunt Ethel told her quite definitely that they came down from Heaven. Having got this clearly in her mind, on one particularly trying day Evelyn declared she wished God would take them back again!

Much later, when we were all children together sharing a holiday, Evelyn boasted to me in bed one night that the triplets had been born within five miles of a lion's den. The picture conjured up in my mind the possibility of a lioness carrying off baby after baby in its mouth to feed its own – oh dear, it *was* hard to get to sleep that night.

THE FAMILY

Well, after that dramatic interlude concerning "the trips" we will return to our own sheltered life in Sussex. Having referred to several members of our long family, perhaps it would clarify matters to put them down in chronological order and give some reason for their names. In the case of the younger members of the family I remember the great discussions that took place before a name was finally decided upon. It was a matter of great importance; there was a strong clannish feeling about the family and many people to be remembered. An infant might remain nameless several weeks before a decision was made.

George Woods, the eldest, was named after Mother's father who had died when she was a little girl. Herbert Procter was named after Father (Herbert) and a brother of his, or more likely after a branch of the family in bygone days, the Procters. We always called Herbert Procter "Bertel" after Bertel Thorvaldsen the Danish sculptor.

Jonathan, the third boy, could have no second name. It was clear he was named simply after our revered paternal grandfather Jonathan Hutchinson, F.R.S. In my mind at least, Grandfather came second only to God. Father was entirely devoted to him and his broad, enlightened philosophy of life. We called our Jonathan, Jan. Rightly or wrongly I connected this with the heroic Dutch story of "Jan and the Windmill."

Christopher West – by now we could begin to introduce new first names, which, like new blood, are good things. One of the aunts (there were many) told Mother that of course he would be Luke as he was born on St Luke's day, but in Mother's mind there was no "of course" about it. There was some confusion, however, as to whether he was named after the new church then being built in Haslemere – St Christopher's – or the church after him. Neither, I feel sure. Our parents would delve far deeper than that to the kindly Saint Christopher who carried the Infant Jesus across the river. We were early shown pictures of this on Sunday evenings. West was our paternal grandmother's maiden name. Amongst ourselves we usually shortened Christopher to Kit, again not without some confusion – for the pony was *Kit* also.

Then I came along, Margaret Massey, both family names. I have always liked my first name. There is no false modesty in me.

Hugh Bernard – again Hugh brought in new blood. Bernard was the name of Father's youngest brother who died at the age of ten. He had been playing in the gardens at Cavendish Square where they lived, when he fell and grazed his knee. Tetanus set in and it must have been a heartbreak for his learned medical father to watch helplessly his little boy sicken and die in ten days. There was no cure.

Alice Mary was after a cousin of our parents who had died shortly before Mary made her entry into the world. I have always thought Mary the most perfect girl's name, and do not think we ever shortened it. It is so simple, so complete.

Rachel remained some while without a name while there was much to-ing and fro-ing. Finally she became Elizabeth after Mother and *her* mother, and Rachel for tears at the death of this maternal grandmother, a few days after Elizabeth Rachel was born. For some years however, she was known in the family as Libby.

Laurence has already been explained. He had no other name. We were dried up.

"DOWNSTAIRS"

Downstairs, though vividly remembered, seems unimportant. When one was not getting up or going to bed one spent all the time possible out of doors and that will play an important part in subsequent chapters.

The stairs were narrow and steep and had a curious bend half way up. Ascending candles cast eerie shadows. It was a recurrent nightmare that I was falling down them, not going bump, bump from stair to stair, but floating through air. I woke with a start just before crashing on to the floor at the bottom. Another reminiscence is of Mary when a toddler picking up a bumble bee on the stairs with disastrous results. As Mother cuddled her on her knee and held the bluebag to the swelling finger Mary wailed – "But I thought it was a buffalode." The bottom few steps were by a window where we sat struggling into boots and leggings or gaiters. We never wore shoes out of doors, though sometimes sandals in the summer. As we were allowed to run anywhere and get our feet very wet we usually wore heavy leather boots. Girls' boots were longer in the leg than boys' and needed more doing up; I often wore boys' boots. They were tiresome to lace, especially if the little metal tip to the lace had come off, then you bent over and licked the frayed end to make it into a point to go through the eyelet. Some boots had hooks around which the laces wound. These were easier, but the hooks had a way of bending and breaking.

Leggings or gaiters, worn in winter, covered our woollen stockings with felt or soft leather. These were generally buttoned with what seemed like an endless stream of horrid round buttons that had to be pulled through the button holes with a button hook. As you reached the fattest part of the calf of your leg you were apt to pinch the skin. I took a great dislike to these last few stairs on which one had to learn the art of lacing and tying and buttoning.

At the bottom of the stairs was a door into a small cobbled yard with a parapet wall and a few steps down on to the big yard, which was really our drive. But in the little yard, just opposite the door were the earth closets – three of them in a row, dark and earthy. We were used to them, but I am glad now that they are a thing of the dim past.

The hall was quite large but unpretentious with dirty shoes and garden coats about.

At the modern end of the house were the dining and drawing-rooms with a passage between leading to the front door.

The dining-room was dominated by one large table with chairs for the family, for we always had meals with our parents after the age of about five. There was a large armchair beside the fire. This has stuck firmly in my mind since the day when I was called in from the garden to see – or be seen by – my uncle the doctor, or doctor my uncle. I quite liked him. He was rather jolly in fact, but I am sure I should have liked him better if he had not been my doctor, and I do not think relatives ought to be doctors, if you get my meaning.

Anyway, on that morning, he sat me up at the dining table and asked Mother to fetch a pudding basin. He then pushed a paint brush down my throat till I retched horribly, poked something else down, pulled out nasty bloody stuff into the basin, and Hey Presto, my tonsils had been removed. He laughed at me for spitting in his face, told Mother I would not like anything salty for a day or two, and departed. I curled up in the armchair and sulked, wondering why I should be made to feel ill when I had been enjoying myself playing in the garden – and that was that.

Father's study, where he did much of his planning of houses, was half very light, with a pretty, low window surrounded by roses and hollyhocks, and half very dark. It must have been part old, dark with blackened beams, and part new where the window was. We used to climb in and out of the window, using it much as one would use a french window. Though this was definitely a "quiet room" (we had a great respect and some awe for Father which perhaps grew as we grew older), he was not at all exclusive about it and enjoyed our company in small numbers.

When I was only a few months old he was planning a beautiful house for Commander Henderson. This house was called Keffolds and has since become well known as a Dr Barnardo Home and later an Ockenden Venture Home. Commander Henderson would come to Father's study and discuss plans and was amused one day to see a baby lying in a rocking cradle in the study. That baby was me.

It shows how, although so intent on his work and his very highbrow interests, Father was a very homely man.

Actually the cradle, though it looked old, was only made up of old oak panels that Father had got hold of somewhere and had put together in his builders' workshop. We did not use it much for babies, but later spent much time playing in it.

THE KITCHEN AND ITS UTENSILS

The kitchen was in the old part of the house, a large rectangular room with a black range at one end and the washing-up sink along one side. This was unusual in those days when washing up was generally done in a pantry or a scullery. One had to pass through the kitchen to get to the back door and the dairy, and this must have made it an awkward room to manage. I am sorry to say my recollection of both kitchen and kitchen staff is that they were rather drear.

It must have been difficult to keep kitchen quarters clean in those days, so many things were dirty anyway. Coal and wood to carry, lamps and candles to see to, knife sharpening, continual drying of heavy wet clothes and boots, for we had no easily dried mackintoshes and no wellington boots. Galoshes were not a practical proposition in the country. They had a habit of staying in the mud as you drew your booted foot out.

Dinner knives were sharpened and stains removed on a flat stone on which a paste of red fuller's earth was spread. They were, of course, washed both before and after. How different from the labour saving stainless steel we have had in use so long now.

The outside of the kettle was always black, though frequently brushed to get the soot off. We often boiled a kettle in the dining-room and on the bars of the fireplace in both this and the drawing-room were fixed circular trivets on which to stand the singing kettle.

A kettle-holder was always kept handy. Cross-stitch kettle-holders, as well as iron-holders, were common presents made by small daughters (in my case under much protest and pressure) as Christmas and birthday presents for one's Mother.

Irons were literally made of iron. They were black and were heated on the kitchen range. To test whether the iron was hot enough one spat on its base. If it fizzed it was just right. Two irons were in use at a time, one heating up as the other was used. They soon cooled and had to be re-heated. A cloth was kept handy to wipe them, for they might well be dirty standing there on the range. Later one was able to buy a stainless metal "shoe" in which to place the iron and this made it much cleaner. It is quite astonishing to realise now how clean and white and well-starched aprons, maids' caps, table-cloths, serviettes, etc all came out. A great deal of hard work went in to the washing (with hard soap) and ironing of all these, as well as our clothing, including long baby gowns. No "drip dry" then.

DOMESTIC STAFF

Though we lived quite comfortably at Moses Hill, ours was not in any way a smart set-up. We generally had a cook and a maid in the kitchen, a nurse or mother's help around, and sometimes a boot-boy who did all kinds of odd jobs. I do not think we always had this number of staff however, for I remember my brothers early being taught to clean shoes, and my being coerced into helping too.

One boot-boy we loved dearly. He was Edgar Head from Fernhurst, a lad of about fourteen. He came up on a bicycle. He must have pushed it most of the way up for Moses Hill was 500 feet sheer above the village but he would have had a grand spin homewards at the end of the day. Edgar was the essence of good nature to us children, and we treated him as a real friend. Later he became chairman of the Fernhurst Parish Council.

For most of the time our nurse was Phoebe, the daughter of Mr and Mrs Wheeler. She ruled the younger members of the family a bit hard, but I, being rather betwixt and between, came off fairly well, and was really quite fond of her.

THE GUTTERING CANDLE

George and Margaret posed for a photograph

PLAYING IN THE GARDEN

"Let us climb up the rockery and sit on the garden wall,"
said Moppet.
They turned their pinafores back to front, and went up with a
skip and a jump.
Beatrix Potter. From *The Tale of Tom Kitten*
Courtesy: Frederick Warne, London

I generally had boys to play with (Kit and Jan)

PLAYING IN THE GARDEN

FATHER'S GARDEN

Father was essentially a planner and creator. He saw opportunities for creativeness where most people were blind. He carved mantle-shelves and door panels, he painted pictures. When he died at the age of eighty-eight he left two thousand unframed watercolours, and the walls of our house were loaded with framed pictures. Many too had been given away in his lifetime.

At Moses Hill, when he was a comparatively young man he created a most enchanting garden covering some two acres, in which we played unsupervised by the hour.

The front door opened into the garden as did another nearby which had a small verandah. This was furnished with a seat round the wall and a table, and one could play at indoor occupations such as puzzles, painting or dolls and still be in the fresh air.

Opposite this was grass and steps and little dry stone walls supporting narrow flower borders. One jumped down the steps, hop, hop, hop, to a wide path that ran along the hillside. In the middle of the path at a point where it had been widened out was an old stone mill-wheel with a sundial on it. It was open and sunny here but the path stretched away on either side under long rose pergolas like tunnels. Rambler roses with such delightful names as *Dorothy Perkins* and *Hiawatha* grew abundantly over the archways.

After leaving the southern pergola the path ran gently down through the orchard and into the wood. It ended at the flattened base of a quarry from which stone had been taken when the Marley Heights road was made just below. Father had engineered this scenic road also.

THE RAILWAY

Bertel and Christopher, however, engineered a railway system. The path was the track, a wheel-barrow the train. I was the passenger. The boys must have worked very hard manually, digging a trench along the side of the path, and laying land-drains through which to pass the string to work the signals. This was an elaborate system involving cotton-reels, posts and bits of boarding; much hammering and painting. Everything that was needed could be found and scrounged from the house and the barns.

There were three stations, one by the shed at the north end of the path, one at the sundial and a terminus down in the quarry. The boys explained to me the meaning of the word 'terminus'.

Hugh and Mary were too little to be trundled at a gallop down the stony path in a rough, splintery barrow, but I loved it. There would be a shrill whistle, a great chug-chugging as Bertel got up steam and Kit worked the signals, which did not always operate according to plan.

There were unavoidable delays caused by technical hitches such as gravel in the land-drain, or the string breaking. But it was all part of the day's work for the boys. I doubt if I did much to help.

The signals must be worked properly by pulling the string, though it would only be a matter of a few yards' walk to operate them by hand.

At last we would be off, through one rosy tunnel, pulling up at the Sundial Station, off again into the comparative darkness of the second tunnel, and out into the sunny orchard where we gathered bumpy speed as we careered down into the wood, and drew up with much puffing and blowing at the terminus.

How to turn round? That was the question. It was much too simple just to wheel the barrow around. A turn-table must be constructed like the one we sometimes saw slowly rotating a real steam-engine at Guildford Station. Home we went to find all we needed and the work began. A shallow circular pit was dug into which the boys placed an old cart-wheel flat down. The details of the mechanism escape me, but when the plank had been nailed on to the hub of the wheel the whole thing could be turned. The barrow was wheeled on to the plank and gently rotated. It stuck.

More earth must be removed from underneath. Kit and Bertel were busy on this when the catastrophe happened. Bertel was moving earth away with his hands while Kit chopped at the roots with the "bill'uk." There was a yell and Bertel pulled his hand away with the first joint of one finger missing. We were horrified.

I do not know which boy suffered most. We rushed home. Edgar

Head was packed off on his bicycle the two miles to fetch Uncle Roger, the doctor, while Mother did what she could by way of first-aid. Poor Kit cried his eyes out. I expect I cried too as I sat in a forlorn and helpless heap nearby. It made a lasting impression on me not least when doctor sent Edgar down to the wood to look for the missing joint. I was glad it was not found.

The wound was stitched up and healed well, and I do not think Bertel suffered much inconvenience from the shortened finger. So much for that game.

GARDEN DESIGN

The garden was a place of many parts. To the south of the house was a large lawn and a long herbaceous border. I looked out onto this when I sat up in bed each morning. It is funny the little unimportant incidents one remembers. Every afternoon I was sent to rest on my bed, which was irksome. I think I spent most of the time kneeling up looking out of the window. The delphiniums were particularly tall and beautiful. One day, seeing Mother out there I got up and ran down to her in my stockinged feet to ask if I might get up. "Well, you seem to be up," she answered. I felt slightly snubbed, but I won anyway, and returned to put on my shoes.

In the making of the Marley Heights road, stone had been quarried as near as possible to where it was needed. One of these quarries was actually in the garden. It was not far from the fruit-cage, but one did not see it until one was actually there.

Father, ever inventive, created a rock-garden in it and up the steep slope at the back of it wound a narrow pathway to a fairy castle. This was only a small platform with a seat and a dry stone parapet wall to keep one from falling down. I would climb up here and sit surveying my little world. Below wound tiny, overgrown paths among rocks covered in bosses of aubrietia, saxifrage, alyssum and other common cushion plants, alive with bees and butterflies. It was a riot of colour, untidy no doubt and intermingled with wild flowers from the meadow nearby, but a delight in its wholeness and isolation.

The lawn was designed to be large enough for tennis but few of us were old enough yet. Croquet was sometimes played and a little desultory cricket and tip-and-run. It was probably a disappointment to some of our aunts and uncles that we were not more keen on games, for they were. Aunt Kitty was a gym teacher and one of the first women over-arm bowlers in cricket. She tried to smarten us up, but to no avail.

EARLY PHOTOGRAPHY

Aunt Kitty took all our family photographs for she was an excellent photographer. She would visit us with her large plate camera and tripod, and pose us in all sorts of positions. Some were certainly attractive such as sitting on a gate or feeding the rabbits, but others, to my mind even then, rather ridiculous. The lawn was a favourite "posing place". The light was good and that was very important in those days, and backgrounds could be simple or even faded out. So out would come a garden chair and George in his new white flannels and school blazer would be seated with me up against him, holding hands. How ridiculous, I thought! We *never* held hands. I *never* sat on his knee! All the same now I must admit the picture is quite pleasing. The most ridiculous photographs, of course, were those showing us playing cricket. There is dear little Hugh, large felt hat on the back of his head and a sweet smile, holding a large bat in the correct position as he eagerly awaits the yorker or whatever that is coming to him. Behind the stumps, which have no bails, stands three-year old Mary, frilly knickers below her frock, looking equally amused and utterly innocent of what it is all about.

Aunt Kitty tried to smarten us up.
My four big brothers posed as (Quaker!) sailor boys

But the photo I always took exception to was taken the same day and shows us all as a cricket team. I cannot say "eleven", for we were only eight *in all*. There stands George, centre back, obviously the captain, *holding a baby* (Rachel), *in long white robes*. On either side are Christopher in a starchy white collar, and Jan who is trying to hide a smile. Kit holds his cricket bat as if he were just going out shooting. Bertel sits next to me. We both hold enormously long-handled bats and look extremely bored, as indeed we were, for the group has taken a long time to arrange.

Behind the stumps stands three-year old Mary
looking as amused and innocent as Hugh

Hugh occupies a large basket chair sitting very erect, still with his bat, determined not to let the side down. Mary is the only happy one. She stands centre clutching her teddy bear and smiling coyly. I suppose I was nine at the time, but not too young to feel cynical about the whole set-up. I am afraid I even felt Aunt Kitty was behaving in a rather ridiculous way as she kept bobbing in and out from under a large black cloth draped over the back of the camera. This is unkind of me for we were very fond of gentle Aunt Kitty and it is entirely due to her that we have many charming photos to remind us of those happy days "before the war". Let us, then, write-off cricket.

PASTIMES

Although I revelled in boyish play and generally only had boys to play with, my sisters being much younger, I was cautious and fearful of being hurt. Amongst other things I hated being upside-down, and never learnt to do "head-over-heels". The Trips, Betty, Fred and Frank, being small and lithe would turn "cart-wheels" over and over all across the lawn. You never knew which way up they would be next. For me, so long as my head went first I did not mind how or what I climbed: fences, gates, haystacks and trees. There was a certain fir tree up which I climbed to what seemed an incredible height, almost in the sky in fact! It was "my" tree and I told no one about it.

Around the yards and the winding paths I would trundle my hoop. At first this was a wooden one with a stick. Such things were easily bought in toy shops and most children had them. As I grew bigger I begged for an iron one, and one was made specially for me by the blacksmith at Fernhurst. Being heavier it went faster, and instead of hitting it along I hooked it with an iron hook set in a wooden handle. It spun along and could be steered with the hook. It would go just as fast as I could run and give me hours of pleasant exercise all alone.

FRUIT PICKING

Over beyond the lawn and its lovely flower border were vegetable beds and a large fruit enclosure. In it were rows of red, black and white currants, raspberries and strawberries.

In season we would spend much time helping Mother to pick fruit. Sometimes Aunt Kitty and Aunt Hilda would come over on their bicycles from Inval, three miles away, to spend the afternoon with us. They would take a basketful home for there always seemed plenty for all.

One day as Aunt Hilda, who was full of fun, was picking along one side of the raspberries a little voice from the other side said cheekily, "Hullo Hilda". It was Christopher. We were very properly brought up to call members of the older generations aunt, uncle, or cousin so-and-so, and Kit was feeling very bold and puckish, (with a good thick hedge between) in addressing an aunt without her proper label. The rule when picking soft fruit was "one in ten, no more," and I think we kept fairly well to this, counting the berries as we picked and popping number ten into our mouths. I was very shocked therefore when a girl who came to tea one day suggested as we went out to play, that we should raid the fruit enclosure.

Perhaps a large family, like a tribe, develops its own code of conduct through popular opinion amongst its members. The rule about eating fruit was, I am sure, of our own making and not imposed from above. It ensured that no-one was over greedy. In passing the fruit cage we were not above helping ourselves to two or three berries, but to go there deliberately to eat – was just not done.

Griselda was an only child and was perhaps missing out on something very valuable in life.

Anyway, Griselda being our visitor that afternoon it was hard to refuse, and I did as she said feeling horrid inside. I have hated the name Griselda ever since.

As a large family we were very self-sufficient and were not anxious for the companionship of other children. Griselda had been foisted on me because she was staying nearby and Mother thought it would be hospitable to ask her in. Perhaps she thought too that it would broaden my outlook.

FURTHER REFLECTIONS

There are certain disadvantages as well as advantages to a large family. On the whole the latter far outweigh the former and despite differences of opinion and changes in religious and political outlook as we grew up we have remained a united family.

One disadvantage as far as I was concerned was that I was so satisfied with my own life within the shelter of the clan that I was shy, perhaps even gauche, with outsiders. There was a ridiculous incident when, at the age of eight, I entirely failed to cope with a simple situation. Modern children will hoot at this!

I was invited to tea with a lady and her daughter about my own age who were staying in a Guest House just down the hill at Kingsley Green. As I ran down I wondered how I should introduce myself. I knocked at the door and a maid in a starched cap and apron opened it. I was struck dumb. I could not possibly say – "I've come to tea," and there seemed nothing else one could say. So we looked at each other and then I turned and ran home.

Mother scolded and said what a silly little goose I was, but no one told me what I should have said, and I have wondered ever since.

We have strayed from the garden to which this chapter is supposed to be concerned. This is inevitable because the garden itself strayed off in all directions, merging into fields, and woods and the farmyard with its magnificent barns. And talking of unsociability there was a day when three of us hid up in the hay-loft, deaf to the calls of Miss

Mathew. ("Matoo" was then our "Mother's Help".) We stayed until such time as we reckoned it would be too late for us to be taken out to tea. We surrendered then but were hurried into best clothes with much scolding while Mother and the pony-trap waited. We went *against* our wills but probably *for* our social training. I forget the rest of the story, perhaps just as well.

Yes, there is no doubt that I at least was happiest in a serge frock or skirt and jersey (worn till the elbows could be patched no more) free as a colt within our wide acres.

It was an understood thing that the toddler of the day would get lost at least once in its toddler-time. There would be a great hue and cry, we scattered and searched and the straying babe, who was never far away, was lovingly and laughingly led home. Most likely Phoebe gave it a quiet smack in the nursery. For the rest of us it added a little more excitement to life in which we made our own amusements and enacted our own personal dramas. There was no T.V. to do it for us.

Mary was an independent little girl, and wandered off one day, causing us great concern, which some of us certainly enjoyed. She was found sitting composedly in the orchard, fat little hands resting on plump knees, contemplating the scene. She was probably glad to be alone awhile whatever the consequences.

Actually there were two orchards, for besides the one through which Bertel and Christopher's railway ran, there was another pleasant sloping area with a clump of hazel bushes at the bottom. These covered what was reputed to be a glass-blowing foundry. Amongst the mossy stones in this little spinney were lumps of siliqua, shining like black glass. That is all we ever knew about it.

Sometimes, it generally seemed to be on a Sunday afternoon, Father would summon up a regiment of children and line us up along the edge of a ploughed field. Then we all moved forward slowly, hunting for flint implements of ancient British manufacture. Few good pieces were found but scrapers, needles, cores and firestones were quite often picked up. The firestones were easily recognisable as they were whitened, cracked lumps of flint that had been burnt white-hot in a fire and then dropped into water to heat it.

Our sandstone hill-top was foreign to natural flint so we knew that every bit we found had been brought there by man, probably by Stone-age man who had walked with it from the South Downs where flint abounded naturally.

As a child it was the searching and discovering that appealed to me; it was much later that I appreciated the full significance. As a student in Training College the "liveness" of our contact with Natural History and country crafts in early youth slipped into place to bring deeper meaning to studies that were often dead to girls who were less fortunate in their early upbringing. Scattered and uncohesive my knowledge may have been but it illustrated the fact that children's minds are receptive to a very wide range of interests and learn a great deal "by the way." When eventually I had my own little Froebel school hidden in the woods just below Moses Hill this practical child-like approach was shared again with a new generation of children.

The word *dolmen* came early into my vocabulary when Father found a very large rock just beneath the turf at the point we called The South Seat. Thinking that it might be something of prehistoric significance he put labourers on to excavate around it. Presently a long rounded rock like the back of a whale was exposed and Father thought it might be a dolmen which the dictionary tells me is a megalithic tomb: that is to say a stone-covered grave, obviously in a place like that, of great antiquity. He sought advice on it but in the end the conclusion was that it was quite natural. It was left open and we children used to clamber about and sit astride it. Later it formed an interesting feature in the rock garden of a house that was built nearby.

Well, this is a mixed-up chapter. But, like childhood itself, it reflects the varied diet of order and disorder and of exploration, not in the sense of discovering far-off places but understanding and appreciating our immediate environment.

How fortunate we were indeed to have such richness and diversity and parents who unobtrusively aided and abetted our play-way of learning. Often they seemed hardly to be there at all, but as our horizons widened they took a more active part as will be seen as this story unfolds.

It is wonderful what can be found in old barns

ON THE FARM

"A snug thack house, before the door a green,
Hens on the midding, ducks in the dabs are seen,
On this side stands a barn, on that a byre …"
… Such picturesque beauties pass not unnoticed by the
young naturalist; their charms invite his first attentions.

Thomas Bewick

Mr and Mrs Wheeler with Phoebe and Leo standing behind.
The boys are grandsons.

ON THE FARM

A HOLY PLACE

Often as I have read the classics such as Dickens or books about country life in the past, or even hymns, I have pictured scenes taking place in one or other corner of this simple hill-top home. Such is the indelible impression it has made on my mind.

For instance, there is the spot where "The Shepherds watched their flocks by night." It was at the top of the field behind the shed where the pig-swill was boiled. From there they would see a fine expanse of sky, plenty of room for the Heavenly Host. I must have been very young when this impression was formed for we only kept sheep for a short time.

Father was not really a farmer and he employed George Parvin, helped spasmodically by Mr Wheeler, to look after a few cows and pigs. George Parvin walked three miles from Inval to work each morning. He had to be up at Moses Hill in time to harness *Kit* the pony in the tub gig (or trap as we usually called it) and drive Father and such of the boys who were old enough down to Haslemere to the office and school respectively. They generally walked home at the end of the day, and very tired the boys were, especially at the last pull up to the top of the hill.

SELF SUFFICIENCY

We had, of course, our own milk and butter and bacon, as well as eggs and chickens. There were quite a number of hens with a cock or two to scratch about the roughly cobbled yard outside the cottage end of the house. This very old part I must describe in some detail for I have very fond memories of its picturesqueness and for Mr and Mrs Wheeler who were our nearest neighbours. It was a biggish square yard with low sheds along the side opposite the house.

The fowls roosted in the sheds and were supposed to lay their eggs in the nest-boxes put there for the purpose. But sometimes a clutch of eggs would be found under the haystack down in the field, or in the hedge, or in a dark corner of the yard. We loved looking for eggs and if we found a dozen together in a neat round hollow made by the hen we were delighted. On occasion a hen would absent herself for about three weeks, appearing in the morning to be fed (we scattered grain all about the Wheeler's yard) and then vanish again. Then one day she would come clucking proudly forth from somewhere along the hedge with a dozen or more fluffy yellow chicks around her.

Every year broody hens were "set" on eggs so that the stock was kept up with chicks that either quickly developed neat little tails and turned into hens, or remained fluffy at the back end until the finer, longer curved feathers of a cockerel appeared.

Mother devoted much care to her sitting hens, often having them cooped with a run for the chicks, in some quiet part of the garden. Right on into the 1950s Mother continued to keep a few hens. Alas, the stringency of food rationing in the second World War did not allow the keeping of a cock so breeding our own had to be abandoned, and she took to buying "point-of-lay" hens. All the fun had gone out of it by then.

At the top of the yard was a square wooden building with tiled roof that housed the well. We were not encouraged to go in there as the well was very deep, but of course we did. And curiosity did *not* kill the cat. We all developed a healthy thirst for knowledge of the world about us encouraged by this free and easy way of life, and we learnt to be careful.

Beneath the spread of a fine ash tree was the dairy with its cold slate slab, the separator for separating milk from cream, the cooler and the churn in which Mother herself generally made the butter. Splosh, splash, splosh, went the cream as she turned the barrel over and over, the sploshes and splashes becoming softer and more bumpy sounding as time went on. Presently she would open the top of the churn and we would see lumps of butter floating in the watery curds. A few more turns and the lumps would coalesce into one large conglomeration which was then taken out between two butter pats and put on to a ridged piece of wood like a draining board. It was kneaded and pressed as the last of the curds were squeezed out and ran down the runnels. Then the butter was cut into rough rectangles and patted into neat shapes rather like the half pounds we buy in the shops now, but generally larger. Always there were lines on the butter made by the pats. We also made little round ridged knobs of butter, rolling them between the pats, for individual helpings at table, and these would appear – a whole dishful – at breakfast and tea-time. It was fun helping to make them and much more useful than messing about with plasticine.

EXPLORATION

It was amongst the roots of the ash tree that I one day decided to dig down to Australia. I must have been an incredibly credulous child, born with the motto "to travel hopefully is better than to arrive."

Someone was teaching us something by them. I know we had a series of governesses, but of lessons I remember practically nothing, which considering I later became a teacher "just goes to show," doesn't it. Anyway, I had been impressed by the fact (interpreted to me in very simple language by one of my brothers) that if you dug far enough you would come out at Australia. I was quite undaunted by the warning that on the way I should have to pass through the fiery furnace that formed the centre of the globe. (Was this Hell, I wondered?). This I knew in my somewhat muddled manner, for better, for worse, for fact or for fiction.

So, with my little sea-side spade I began to dig. It was particularly rooty under the ash tree and I did not get far, perhaps a foot or two, when I began to tire. I struggled on a little longer and lo and behold struck coal. This exciting discovery (for I also knew about coal mines, my brothers having been taken down one by Father who believed in practical demonstration), gave me an excellent excuse for abandoning Australia. I rushed indoors with my news, but no one seemed particularly interested. I expect I was sent to wash my hands for tea or something like that, and I concluded later that at some time someone had dumped a load of coal under the ash tree.

THE WHEELERS

The Wheeler's yard, of course, led to the Wheeler's cottage, with a low doorway leading into a real old cottage parlour. We would run in to call on Mrs Wheeler whenever we liked, usually in my case when I felt out of favour elsewhere. She was a dear little elderly Sussex woman, dressed in black or grey with starched apron, and smiling, wrinkled face that had I known Beatrix Potter's books then, I should have recognised as Mrs Tiggy-Winkle.

How we loved to get into the chimney corner by her huge log fire. There was a seat on each side, and if you could, safely, without getting burnt, peer up the chimney you could see the sky.

In the lower part of the chimney were shelves for smoking bacon. Over the fire hung a chain with a large black kettle. Mrs Wheeler always made us welcome and there was something particularly attractive about the scrubbed simplicity of her room with its rag rug and patchwork cushions.

As I said, it was to Mrs Wheeler that one repaired to lick one's sores; not to tell tales, but just to forget.

Alas, I could not stomach porridge, the staple breakfast food of those days long before cereals were invented. Every morning I sat over my bowlful as the gooey stuff grew colder and more glutinous. When the rest of the family got up from breakfast I was sent to the nursery to finish it. One day, after a particularly nauseating session I slipped round to Mrs Wheeler, entered her door and was promptly sick all over her well scrubbed brick floor.

Without a word of admonition she fetched pail and cloth and cleaned it all up while I watched in abject misery. She must have put in a kindly word for me at home, for from that day I was excused porridge.

Mr Wheeler was a bearded country man in stout corduroy trousers tied beneath the knee, and baggy coat with large pockets from which could issue either a live ferret or a dead rabbit. Besides gardening and doing odd jobs about the place his main occupation was charcoal burning in the good old-fashioned way which will be described later on.

Hugh remembers that Mr Wheeler told us tales of his youth; that he could remember the stage-coach trundling along the road before the railway was made and that he saw Richard Cobden who lived at Heyshott. He would have good reason to remember the Repeal of the Corn Laws in 1847 for his family was so poor that they ate pig food when they could not afford bread. He left school at the age of seven and it is doubtful if he could read and write much. On his death in 1937 at the age of ninety-four his obituary in the local paper filled in for us gaps in our memory of this grand old Sussex character.

As children we liked old Tom Wheeler and were merely amused at his somewhat fatalistic attitude towards his own life which was quite unwarrantable.

When the older boys were of an age to go to boarding school they never left without going to say good-bye to the Wheelers.

"Goodbye, Mas'er George, goodbye, Mas'er Jan," he would say in his deep voice through that shaggy grey beard, "You won't see me no more. I shan't be 'ere when you comes 'ome." But he always was, and lived many years after we left Moses Hill.

Talking of goodbyes, my brothers also went three miles to say goodbye to Grandfather. It was well worth while. Putting his hand in his pocket he would pullout a small coin. "Is that a farthing or a half sovereign, George?" he would ask, "Your eyes are better than mine." It was, of course, a gold half sovereign, a "tip" for the school-boy.

Although Mr and Mrs Wheeler always used a prefix to our names – Miss Margaret, Master Christopher, etc, and we always referred to Mrs Wheeler, on one occasion I was severely reproached by Phoebe for referring to "Wheeler" as Father always did. "My father has a handle to his name just as much as yours," she sternly reminded me.

FARM LAYOUT AND EQUIPMENT

There were in actual fact four "yards" at Moses Hill besides the large garden. We always called the large grassy patch with the circular driveway round it "the yard". To use the word driveway is to give a false impression of those whose memories go no further back than tarred surfaces. There were no tarred roads then, and our drive was merely an earthen track round a patch of short turf. Even this could not be described as "lawn". It was all quite unpretentious as a front entrance to a house but pleasant in its simplicity and spaciousness.

On the side of this large yard opposite the house was a magnificent old barn with massive oak beams and struts all hand cut and showing the marks of axes perhaps five hundred years old. Large double doors opened into the centre of the barn and hay waggons could draw in from one side, unload, and draw out through another pair of doors into the farmyard beyond.

Hay was stored on one side of the barn and it was delicious to climb up into it, and in the semi-darkness make a nest into which to snuggle down, perhaps to play houses, to plot some escapade or just to hide from whoever was likely to want us.

On the other side of the barn were stored other feeding stuffs for the animals, and there were three man-handled machines: the mangold crusher, the hay cutter and the tool sharpener. There were no mechanical cutters. All these were either manipulated by turning a handle or by a foot treadle. We kept the sharpener with us for many years, taking it when we moved to other homes. It was a solid wheel of stone some eighteen inches across set in a wooden frame about chest height, and rotated by foot pedal.

With one foot working the pedal and both hands steadying the blade, tools such as scythes, sickles, bill-hooks (bill'uks the men called them) choppers and axes were ground to a fearsome sharpness.

Behind Hugh is the big barn where we often played

For re-sharpening while in use in the field or at the wood stacks a hone was used. This was made of carborundum, measured about a foot long, was rounded and slightly tapered at each end. It was easily broken if dropped, and it was not safe to use a broken piece because one might find one was sharpening the tool on one's hand by mistake. Scythes and sickles were in constant use and I have often used them myself, not very expertly. The gentle swish of a scythe used by a man of Mr Wheeler's skill is a sight and sound alas gone with so many of the gentle arts. Even lawns were cut by scythe, with a beautiful velvety result. There were many pleasant sounds about a farm that have gone, to be replaced by the screech and tearing of motor and electrically driven high power machinery. These, of course, save an untold amount of time and energy and backache, but fill the countryside with hideous noise.

It is extraordinary to reflect that the only engine we had during the first decade of this century on our hill-top was a little model steam engine mounted on a wooden base. It had a boiler heated by an oil lamp and when the water reached boiling point and steam was given off a wheel rotated. That was all, but it taught us the power of steam. It was sometimes linked to a meccano-made crane and persuaded to wind it up. How different from the electrically and magnetically controlled toys of modern children.

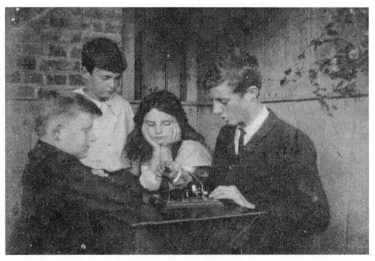

The only engine we had was a little model steam engine demonstrated here by George

Apart from this mechanical innovation we were much more concerned with things we could make with a few bits of wood and some nails and the odds and ends we found in dark corners of the barns. But above all we were concerned with the things of the good earth and our animals.

PETS

We were encouraged to have pets. There were a few cats about, mostly around the farm buildings to keep down rats and mice. No rodent operators or chemical pesticides were needed. We also had an old spaniel, *Jerry.* He lived in a kennel and never came indoors. He had belonged to our doctor uncle who was keen on shooting, but *Jerry* had become rather deaf and gun-shy, so retired to us. He came on walks with us and lived a fairly happy life I think, but was not at all a pet in the sense of the word now-a-days.

Soon after we left our hill-top and moved to a house lower down, Father *did* use some rat poison in the garden and was filled with remorse when poor *Jerry* ate some and died. We gathered in a corner of the garden to bury him and Father was in tears.

Although we children were expected to help to look after our pets I do not think much coercion was put upon us to make us feel really responsible, and none of us have grown up caring much to have animals as pets. For myself I much prefer them in the wild state.

We kept rabbits and enjoyed the litters of baby bunnies that appeared now and then. We spent quite a lot of time gathering greenstuff for them. We called hogweed "Rabbits' Rhubarb". We gave them dandelion leaves in moderation, groundsel, cleavers and vegetable leaves and roots from the garden. They had bran also which we bought along with cow-cake and chicken corn and meal for the pigs, from the corn merchants in Haslemere. There were two shops almost opposite each other at the bottom of Shepherd's Hill and the beginning of the High Street. One never sees a corn merchant in most towns now-a-days. The nearest approach would be a pet shop selling budgie food, peanuts and tins for cats and dogs.

FOOD FOR ALL

I do not think we bought anything in tins, either for animal or human consumption, and certainly nothing frozen. We put down eggs in water-glass (a solution of silicate of soda) when they were plentiful, in large earthenware jars. One just dropped the eggs gently in as one could spare them, and the top ones became coated with white chalky stuff. It washed off quite easily, but water-glass eggs were not fresh enough to eat boiled.

Fruit was bottled, being sealed with fat until screw-top air-tight bottles were obtainable, and much fruit was made into jam. We never bought jam or marmalade. Cutting up Seville oranges was a constant evening occupation in the month or so after Christmas. Apples were stored, and some made into apple rings. I disliked these because, although the core was supposed to have been removed, there was always nasty sharp little bits left in.

Vegetables, of course, were home grown, and there was a goodly selection without such extravagances as asparagus or globe artichokes.

Jerusalem artichokes grew like weeds. They were knobbly and difficult to clean and peel, but made delicious soup.

With so much home-grown produce and the large family to feed there was quite an amount of waste such as vegetable parings and roughage off meat. This was boiled in the special iron boiler in the pig swill shed. Each afternoon a wood fire was lit beneath the cauldron and the smell was curious and pungent to say the least. When thoroughly cooked it was mashed down with a big wooden masher (home-made) and thickened up with meal. But it was still a sloppy mess when buckets-full were poured into the long wooden troughs from which the pigs guzzled noisily after the manner of their kind. We watched with disgusted amusement, and well understood the rebuke occasionally handed out to us at table that we were eating like pigs. I wonder how many modern children know how a pig eats.

One of the boys was not very well. Uncle Doctor had called to see him. He was chatting to him when Mother came into the room and he laughingly told her that he had enquired if he ate well. "I eat alright," was the reply, "but Mother says I don't eat well, I make a noise when I eat."

THE FARM ANIMALS

Behind the big barn that was our joy on wet days were the stables and the cow stalls. The cows were brought in to be milked. In Somerset, to which we repaired during World War One, cows were still being milked out-of-doors, the milker carrying his stool and pail to each in turn as it stood in the field.

Of course, milking was done by hand. I tried mine a few times, but never got the hang of it. I expect I was too small. It certainly seemed quite hard work to entice the milk to flow.

Kit, the pony, was chestnut with black mane and tail, and was not at all an exciting creature. This was just as well, considering that it had to pull a carriage full of small children. Both my parents could drive, of course, and the older boys. Bertel was particularly fond of animals and could harness *Kit,* talking gently to him to get his cooperation.

Catching *Kit* after a spell in the field was always a hazard. He was elusive and wary. He would come gingerly up to the bowl of oats that was offered him, and then duck his head and canter off before the halter could be slipped over his head. How we ever kept appointments with all there was to be done before one actually set off in the trap I cannot now think, and there was no telephoning to say we were delayed. Perhaps whoever was detailed to catch and harness *Kit* was given all the morning to do it. We live at a so much greater pace these days, but how much more do we really achieve? It is always a puzzle to me as I think of the leisurely yet efficient and healthy lives we lived then.

Well, there we are at the end of another chapter. The buildings, the yards, the animals and our nearest neighbours introduced. Except one, our donkey. He will take us, rather unwillingly, along the lanes that were all our own on the top of the hill.

ON THE FARM

Hugh and Mary on Zephyr

OUR HILL TOP

One with our random fields we grow.

Hilaire Belloc

We gathered greenstuff for our rabbits (Hugh and Margaret)

OUR HILL TOP

THE DONKEY *ZEPHYR*

George, Bertel, Jan and Christopher were now old enough to harness donkey and cart and roam the quiet lanes without supervision. I often tagged along with them and we had a great deal of fun.

The donkey was born of *Assolanda* belonging to Grandfather, and when it was old enough to be useful it came up to Moses Hill with the poetic name of *Zephyr,* "because," as the boys explained, "he goes like the wind."

This was frightful sarcasm of course. *Zephyr* only went when prodded with a stick or frightened with the rattle of stones in an old tin can. He went more in gusts than a steady blow, often pausing to graze at the roadside.

Sometimes the boys rode *Zephyr,* but I would risk no such daring. True to donkey nature he could be extremely stubborn. When you asked him to start he stood stock still. If you were just climbing into the cart or were waiting for more of the family to come, he would be off.

The gully was very rough and stony and had high banks. One day Bertel was standing with *Zephyr* harnessed to the donkey-cart at the top when some devil entered the animal's head, and he started off down the bank. Bertel, bless him, hung on to the reins and shouted to try to hold him back, but was dragged down and down till they came to the stone wall that held up the bank. Over went donkey, cart and Bertel, landing upside down in the gully with Bertel under the cart.

By a miracle no more harm was done than a couple of broken shafts. It gave us lots to exclaim about, and Bertel revelled in being the hero of the day.

Father had a habit of buying up "lots" at auction sales so that we accumulated all kinds of junk that came in handy in our play. One was an invalid chaise or bath-chair. The boys careered about with this and I as usual was the passenger. But the greatest fun was to tie the chaise onto the donkey-cart and make *Zephyr* pull the lot. Then some mischievous boy in the cart would unhitch the chaise, leaving it and its occupant stranded in the middle of the road while the jeering cart-load proceeded on its way.

When one considers the state of the roads now-a-days one shudders to think of the consequences of such escapades. But those were glorious days for lively country children who never had to be told to "mind the traffic." Up there on our hill-top we were the traffic.

We boasted that *Zephyr* was the last animal to be impounded in Haslemere. The pound was a small brick enclosure full of nettles at the North end of the High Street, called to this day "Pound Corner." A straying animal well deserved those nettles, I thought.

Well presently, *Zephyr* died. We found him lying in the field with his stomach blown out like a balloon. We said "What did our donkey die of? Eating yew." This was thought to be extremely funny and mitigated our loss.

He was buried in the orchard alongside a horse whose origin I know not, and next year we set to and dug them both up again! The energy of my brothers was great indeed for the graves were large and deep.

The skeletons were clean and white and we placed the skulls with much ribaldry, either side of The Hollow in order to frighten two elegant ladies who lived in the house at the bottom of this little lane. For years I cherished certain bones and teeth, particularly a couple of lumbar vertebrae grown firmly together with osteo-arthritis, as mine are doing. Very interesting!

MY FIRST NATURAL HISTORY

Of course we grew up in ideal surroundings for anyone with a bent for Natural History and my life-long interest must have been awakened almost before I can remember.

There was a little lane just beyond the farm where we often played in a clump of holly trees known to us as "The Holly House." We would scramble in and play "Mothers and Fathers."

Along this lane was a high bank with tree stumps and roots, little holes and crevices, mosses with swans' necks, lichens with fairy cups and sealing-wax, and the fern with the funny name of Polypody. One spring morning Mother, finding me at a loose end, suggested that I should go and look for a robin's nest along the lane. I hunted and hunted, but all in vain. Then Mother came out and found one almost at once. Her gentle, quiet enjoyment as she showed me the five pink-spotted eggs impressed me very much. From then on I seemed to know how to look. Kit and I became ardent birdnesters all through the spring holidays, but it was always Mother who found the willow-warblers' nests, "oven-birds" she called them, deep in a grassy bank.

Mr Wheeler waged war on blackbirds and thrushes, taking all their eggs to eat for his tea. This was because they ate his fruit. Another bird he kept severely in check was the bullfinch which destroyed so many fruit buds during the winter. We considered the bullfinch quite an uncommon bird, and were excited whenever we saw one or found its nest. Kit and I collected eggs, but our rule was always to take not more than one out of a clutch of four or five. We considered it very unsporting to cause a bird to desert its nest.

We blew the eggs, not always very successfully, through a pin-hole at either end, and kept them in cotton-wool in a little cabinet. But I do not think either of us were keen collectors, and child-like, presently grew out of the habit. When I found that mice had played havoc with my rather scatty little collection I decided to call it a day. Bird-watching developed rapidly and became a lifelong hobby, taking first place over all other branches of Natural History.

Another bank near our garden was carpeted with white periwinkles. These all came from a small root Mother had brought back from her honeymoon in Brittany. To each of her several homes she transplanted a little, and now over eighty years later I have it still in my garden.

STARTING AS AN ORNITHOLOGIST

We had few children's nature books. The best of these were several in the "Shown to the Children" series. It was with the help of *Birds shown to the Children* that Christopher and I learnt to identify the birds that seemed so plentiful in those days; such birds as yellow-hammers and linnets, stonechats and whitethroats (nettle creepers they were often called) that abounded in hedgerows that were real hedges, layered and thick, and commons that were not yet grown over with birch and pine, but were sunny and open and colourful. Skylarks, too, nested in the hayfields that are now either left to grow scrub, or are built over. Even the red-backed shrike or butcher-bird nested each year along a certain stretch of thorny hedge.

Another little book that came out in 1910 and which I still possess is *British Nesting Birds* by Percival Westall. This gave brief notes on each bird, arranged alphabetically, definitely a book of reference, certainly the first of its kind I learned to use. In contrast were such books as *Wild Nature won by Kindness* by Mrs Brightwen and Mrs

Catty's *Parables from Nature*. I plodded through stories in such books seeking what information I could, sometimes wallowing in the sentimentality, but seldom seeking spiritual enlightenment.

Different again were books by the Kearton brothers, Richard and Cherry. They were first-rate ornithologists, illustrating their works with photographs. They must have been some of the first to set up hides from which to take close-ups of birds at the nest. The photo of the cow standing stiffly (it was stuffed), gazing into a skylark's nest in the grass was particularly intriguing, for Cherry was hidden inside with his camera lens winking through the cow's eye. These books I read again and again and again. My excitement therefore knew no bounds when Richard Kearton came to Haslemere to give a lantern lecture in the recently built Haslemere Hall. To see a man who had actually written books, to hear his voice and see the slides taken with such patience and often at great risk, filled me with awe. These brothers perhaps more than anyone set me on my determined path towards being a reliable bird-watcher – dare I say it, an ornithologist?

OTHER RECREATIONS

In the summer a large square tent was erected on the lawn in which we held our flower-show, organised by Father as were most of our more intellectual pursuits. We were encouraged to collect and name as many wild flowers as we could, and our two families of cousins, the Edward Roshers and the Roger Hutchinsons, joined in. It was a great day with special cakes for tea. This I remember for the curious quirk I had about chocolate buns. They just would not go down, though they looked so tempting, and chocolate in any form was a rare treat.

I have wandered. Of course tea was only a small item. The show must go on! Though I expect most of the children taking part thought it a bit of a bore, for they were much keener on games such as cricket and tennis, and doing clever things like turning cartwheels, it was just what I enjoyed and consequently remembered clearly.

As the older boys went off to boarding school I was left the eldest at home during term-time. Being the middle one of the brood I had already tasted the freedom of playing with my older brothers who could do so much without supervision, I was now thrown on my own resources. I would climb to the top of my special tree and sing and sing. No-one there to tell me how flat I was, no-one to say "Don't wake the baby."

But, inevitably, I was now linked on to the regime of the nursery at times, and most afternoons was taken for walks with Phoebe, and "the little ones," Hugh, Mary and eventually Rachel. These walks were formal. We set off, Phoebe pushing the pram or the mailcart and those who could walk, doing so quietly beside her. No time now for birds-nesting or scaling a bank to pick harebells. There was a set code of conduct with a corresponding series of punishments attached, to which we became quite familiar. To run ahead or lag behind was penalised by having to hold the pram for a time. If we erred a second time, no cake for tea. A third act of naughtiness meant, of course, no jam. On one occasion I got down to dry bread.

The lanes were metalled with local sandstone, and puddles and rough stones were the accepted thing. Running to catch up to Phoebe one easily tripped over, tearing large holes in the knees of one's hand-knitted stockings and making a bloody mess of the knee itself. The set punishment was meted out. There was no sympathy for the scraped knee-cap, but much scolding for the torn stocking, for Phoebe and Mother always had piles of mending to do in the evenings. I cannot possibly imagine how many pairs of stockings and socks Mother knitted in her life-time.

There was one kind of walk with Phoebe we really enjoyed. On warm summer afternoons we would take a book, often a Louisa Alcott or a *Katy Did* and settle on a mossy bank in the shade and Phoebe would read to us. Even on Sunday afternoons when her young man, Leo, accompanied us, we all settled happily, chewing grass stems as we listened to Phoebe's reading.

Phoebe would take us beyond the confines of our land to Marley Common which was a mass of purple heather and golden gorse with wide views north and south.

SPECIAL OCCASIONS

Three occasions stand out in my memory of special visits to Marley. One was when Father took us after dark on a winter's evening to watch a magnificent display of Northern Lights, the Aurora borealis. A pale pink glow beyond Hindhead gradually deepened to red with flashes of green and yellow, only to fade again. It came and went again and again, silently, awesomely.

To celebrate the coronation of King George V in 1911 bonfires were lit on all the hill-tops. Father and the boys prepared a magnificent one on Marley Common and we all went along when it was dark and lit it up. From there in the glow and warmth of our own fire we counted up how many we could see away over Hindhead and Grayshott and down south to Hollycombe and the South Downs.

Father pick-a- backed a sleepy little girl home after the celebration ended.

Another incident up there is not a happy one; in fact it was a nasty shock. I always knew and accepted that Mr Wheeler and country men of his sort carried a gun and shot rabbits and rats and any birds they disapproved of. But I came up against the real thing in a particularly senseless way when one winter's afternoon I was on Marley with a boy from Kingsley Green and his father. "Gentlefolk" these, I knew. The man was carrying a gun. A flock of tiny birds flew over twittering. Bang went the gun and a lifeless bundle of pretty little feathers lay at our feet. It was a redpoll, the first I had ever seen or heard of – and it was dead. The man and boy seemed to take no more interest in it beyond telling me its name, and I carried it home sadly. This wanton killing haunted me for a long time, and to this day I can remember the exact spot and the circumstances perfectly. Father made a water-colour painting of the little redpoll lying dead which I still cherish, for Father's painting was very sensitive.

I said there were three occasions I remember especially, but a fourth is perhaps worth recounting as it is a further indication of my awakening feeling for natural history.

Soon after leaving Moses Hill but while still living in the vicinity at Kingsley Green I wandered up to the heather alone and sat in a little dip watching the bees at work amongst the flowers. I planned that I would make an out-of-doors laboratory here for the special study of insects. I thought about it a long time, picturing little glass jars hidden in this dell. Whether anyone had told me about the work of Henri Fabre I doubt, but I was thinking just along the same lines.

Alas, I was too young then to know how to begin along scientific lines though there was definitely an urge within to do something original.

No-one put me in the way of this kind of work later on. At school there was no opportunity to learn biology or even botany and the headmaster who taught chemistry and physics was an awesome figure of whom I was terrified. I could see no connection between these studies and the living, pulsating animals and plants I loved so much. The out of school Natural History Society fulfilled my need to a certain extent by giving me the opportunity to share what knowledge I gained by myself. So all my life Natural History has perforce had to take second place, but has proved to be an invaluable hobby.

SCHOOL HOLIDAYS

The return of the boys for holidays added a new dimension to life. Though they seemed different, more grown-up, they had not lost their love of the freedom of our hill-top farm. On several occasions they brought back school friends for a week or two and looking back I can well imagine how much these boys revelled in our simple way of life. Two brothers, Jack and Walter Cheney, who came at different times were the sons of a printer in Banbury and were used to small-town life. What escapades they got up to with Jan who was always full of fun and mischief! They teased Phoebe, of whom the rest of us lived in awe, and Hugh, who was still "in the nursery," remembers how they climbed up the creeper on the wall, through the nursery window, and stole sugar lumps from the tea-table, and went out again before Phoebe could catch them. This kind of joking was, I imagine, generally enjoyed by "the staff," who looked upon school-boys as almost a different species from the youngsters in their care who at all costs must be disciplined.

It was while one of the Cheney boys was staying with us that Jan developed mumps. Telegrams were sent back and forth to Banbury and the holiday was ended abruptly as the boy was reluctantly sent home. In the meantime Jan was isolated in the upper floor of another barn. This was a curious place, barn on the ground floor from which a staircase led up to a second floor only half covering the area. It was rather like a stage only very high up and there was no wall of any kind to prevent one stepping off it into space. However there was another complete room and here a bed was put up for Jan. It was considered quite a joke. Jan would talk to us through the window and lowered a basket into which we put his food. This is how I remember it, but I am sure Mother saw to it that he had more attention than that. The isolation proved ineffective for three of the four other boys caught it in due course. In a large family infectious illnesses could be a great nuisance. There was no inoculation against any of the common ailments, and I spent much of my time when a secondary school girl in quarantine.

Christopher too, brought home two brothers, Leslie and George Ford-Smith, who entered into our life with enthusiasm. Leslie was the happy-go-lucky type who, quite innocently, was only too often finding himself in trouble. If anyone tore their trousers on a rusty nail in the barn it was sure to be Leslie. It was Leslie who fell in the pond, etc, etc. He laughed through all his misadventures while Mother and Phoebe dried and mended his clothes and tried to return him to his parents more or less intact. Many, many years later he visited us with his wife and child. Walking along a lane he innocently picked some hazel nuts, only to be accused of stealing by an irate lady living the other side of the hedge. It was just Leslie's luck!

THE FASCINATING POND

Oh yes, have I mentioned the pond? Up on our hill we even had a *pond.* It was reputed to be a dew pond. It filled a dip in a field, a pretty oval pool some fifty yards long and fifteen wide. For us it filled the need for what educationists call "water-play" and what Kenneth Grahame called "messing about in boats."

George and Bertel in the punt.
The roofs of our farm can be seen against the sky-line.

George says that to stop him from hammering nails into furniture and sawing off bits that should be left on, he was sent down to Haslemere one holiday to learn a bit of carpentry in the workshop of Father's "Haslemere Builders." Here he constructed a punt that was rather like an outsize coffin (without the lid of course). I would think that the carpenter in charge had little more idea of punts than George himself. Anyway it was extremely strong, and it worked, which was all that mattered. Such aesthetics as graceful lines and proportions were of no account to us.

Bare-legged, and in my case with frock and petticoat tucked into bloomers, we waded to the punt and generally paddled about and got extremely wet. No-one seemed to bother about damp clothes. With great care and holding up my clothes as far as ever they would go, I could just paddle across the pond. But more often than not all those holding-up parts got damp and remained so unnoticed till by bed-time they were more or less dry again.

Photographs show the older boys generally in knicker-bockers buttoned just below the knee with long socks with a turndown top patterned in a contrasting colour. Sometimes they wore flannels, grey trousers not at all easy to roll up when punting. The younger boys wore knickers. We should now call them shorts. But they came either exactly to the knee or for some extraordinary reason just below. Often the boys suffered from sores behind the knees due to rubbing of rough serge. Of course as the boys grew the shorts inevitably became shorter.

Sandals were worn in summer and younger children and girls wore socks instead of stockings. In really hot weather it was sandals only and I remember so well constantly stopping to shake stones out of them. On a walk with Father, who always set the pace and disliked too many halts, one would hobble along uncomfortably, trying to get rid of the stone or grit without letting on. In the end one would have to ask to sit down and take the sandal off, but one felt very unpopular. But despite all this over-dressing, play in the pond away from supervision was a great let-off.

A pier was built at one end of the pond, a rickety affair but our own, and not content with George's punt Christopher decided to make a contraption with three tubs. (It is wonderful what old barns and sheds will unearth.) They were nailed together in a bunch and this is when Kit swore. It is wonderful also the language a farm can produce.

The wood was probably teak or oak, anyway it was extremely unyielding and I remember standing holding the tubs in place, as nail after nail bent double and refused to go in. Eventually however, Kit's perseverance was rewarded. The three tubs were together and then with Kit in one, Hugh in another and myself in the third we set off in a slow circular movement, Kit pushing us along as best he could with the punt pole.

Often the triplet cousins, Betty, Fred and Frank, would spend the day getting as wet as we did.

Lying in the field was a large wooden notice board advertising land for sale. We heaved it down to the pond and found two large airtight oil-cans to put under it to keep it afloat. The board had a long post which stuck out behind and did little to help us along. Now we could have Oxford and Cambridge boat races. Three in the tubs and the rest on the raft; one, two, three and we were off! Off was the operative word, for whichever craft got ahead first stayed there as there was no room to pass, unless one pushed the other into the bank.

The raft was all very well so long as the oil-cans stayed in place. Sooner or later, however, one would pop out and go floating away on its own, and the raft sank. Never mind, we would paddle after it and push it back in place again. Afloat once more we would climb on and with much shouting and cheering proceed erratically towards our goal.

To modern children with their sophisticated toys, their swimming pools, Father's yacht on the lake or even on the sea, all this must be a lot of silly nonsense. It did three things however, it cost our parents nothing, it kept us out of their way, and we were never bored. We raced home when called in for meals and were back again at the pond as soon as possible. No questions asked, no accident, no ill-humour that we could not resolve ourselves.

OUR HILL TOP

The woods near Lynchmere in 1879. Little had changed thirty years later when the children ran down the hill to watch the woodcutters.

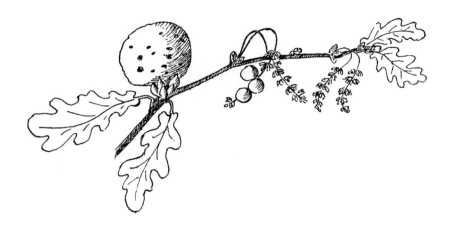

IN THE WOODS

In careless patches through the woods
The clumps of yellow primrose stood,
And sheets of white anemones,
Like driven snow against the trees,
Had covered up the violets,
But left the bluebells bluer yet.

A A Milne. From *When We Were Very Young*
Courtesy: Methuen, London

A woodcutter making barrel hoops
(Photo by MM Hutchinson 1945)

IN THE WOODS

HAUNTS OF THE WOOD-CUTTERS

Around the farm buildings lay the fields, flat and sunny on the hill-top. It was no distance, however, to the steep slopes covered in woodland.

The tracks leading off the hill were all romantic, being deep gullies like the one Bertel and the donkey rolled down, and the Hollow decorated with skulls. Another, even narrower and muddier, led into woods that went on literally for miles to Lynchmere and Hollycombe. This dark tunnel completely overhung by trees we called **The Rabbit Hole**. Surely it was where Alice followed the White Rabbit – into Wonderland.

The darkness ended suddenly in a sunny glade which formed the junction of four paths and tracks trailing off through chestnut coppice. The fascination of this type of woodland lay in its constant change for it was a cultivated crop, sections of which were cut at regular intervals. So one had parts that were newly felled and open to the sky, other parts with young growth a few feet high and so on up to coppice ten or twelve feet above ones head. Chestnut was grown for a variety of purposes. If cut at four years of age the wood was right for walking-sticks which were hand-made over the border in Surrey in small factories at Witley and Chiddingfold. If left to grow a few years longer the straight poles were cut for pit-props for coal mines, or fence posts or bean sticks. Or again they were split to make barrel-hoops and exported to France to the vine-growing areas. Barrels from France were recognised in a local inn as having hoops around them cut in our local woods.

Wood-cutters arrived after leaf-fall and set up their large canvas tents in which to work throughout the winter. First the crop was cut, leaving the stumps to sprout again and send up a number of straight rods for the ensuing years. After trimming off the top and the side shoots the poles were stacked in one corner. A fire burned outside on which a "billy" or a kettle boiled and a pleasant smell of burning prevailed as the blue smoke curled gently up. In fact it was often the sight of smoke in the distance that led us to the wood-cutter.

We children would trot down to the scene of action and watch respectfully. We hardly spoke and certainly never dared to touch anything.

These men of the woods led lonely lives that reminded me of tales of Red Indian trappers whose lives were so solitary they almost lost the power of conversation. Certainly there was none with us. We might be asked the time, which we probably did not know, but that didn't matter, for the wood-man worked the day through, only packing up his shoulder-bag as daylight began to fail. Then he would cover the fire with earth and trudge home sometimes two or three miles, content with a good day's work and the pay that would come the hard way. For his was piece-work. So, when we visited the wood-man we automatically caught onto his quietude and watched intently.

Chestnut splits easily and evenly and the most fascinating operation was that of splitting a pole perhaps six feet long into a number of whippy barrel-hoops by cutting sharply into one end with an adze and then pushing it forward round a peg stuck in one end of the bench on which the woodman sat. Helped by the adze being gently twisted back and forth in the slit the pole soon split right along to the woodman's hand holding the other end. Thus the pole was in half lengthwise. Each half was then split again, and probably several times till the thin slivers were obtained, each with a strip of bark on the outside. We were suitably impressed by the thought that these were going over the seas to France.

Before making fencing, "Fernden fencing" we called it because a local firm of that name bought most of our chestnut, the poles had all their bark removed. It lay in piles, curling up as it dried, and much of it found its way on to the fire outside. Presently our mood of quietness would wear thin, and we would run off home again.

MR WHEELER – THE CHARCOAL BURNER

There was real romance surrounding Mr Wheeler's charcoal burning. I would set off with dear Mrs Wheeler with a basket on her arm covered with a white napkin. Down the Rabbit Hole we went, along the right hand path to a large, flat, circular clearing. Here we were greeted by "Old Wheeler" to many grownups, or "Tom" to his wife, but I was careful always to say "Mr Wheeler" since that day when I had referred to him as "Wheeler."

But what an old-man-of-the-woods he looked there, standing in the clearing. His shaggy beard was as begrimed with smoke as his face and hands. His shirt and jacket too were smeared with black and his baggy, brown corduroy trousers strapped tight beneath the knee with a leather strap, or sometimes just string, bore all the signs of having been lived in many days and nights. We were quite undismayed by this contrast to his neat little wife however, for it was an integral part of his job. "I'm that hungry I could eat a donkey," he would grunt. How *awfully* funny I thought, taking him literally.

The basket was opened to reveal delicious baked pies and pasties, chunks of beef, ham, cheese and bread, and home-made brawn, all so fresh and clean in contrast to the recipient.

Mr Wheeler was spending three weeks in the wood tending the charcoal-making fire. In the centre of the clearing was a large pyramid of chestnut stakes some six feet tall. They were covered with earth and sods beaten down with a shovel. A small amount of smoke wafted out of the top and there was a distinctly sooty smell. Whenever smoke issued out of the side a shovelful of earth was put on it to stop the draught. At the bottom were several small holes inside which I could see red embers. This was all the air that was needed to keep the wood very slowly charring. The whole operation took three weeks for the principle was to char the logs right through without burning them to ashes.

During this time Mr Wheeler was in charge and only when he saw blue smoke coming out of the top did he seal up all the draughts at the base and leave it to cool. Then carefully he would remove the sods and earth and find his wood stack turned to fine sticks of charcoal.

But, visiting him with Mrs Wheeler taking his food for the day there was something else even more intriguing to me as a little girl. This was the little hut which he had built to live in so that he could attend to the fire by night as well as by day, as and when necessary.

It was made of chestnut posts and thatched with flakes and bark from the woodman's craft. Inside was his bed. It consisted of four posts driven into the ground over which was stretched a piece of wire-netting. A thick layer of dead bracken made the mattress, and rugs and sacking the covering. His fire burned outside with a stout wooden tripod over it from which hung his black kettle.

What a life! The idea of loneliness never occurred to me. I just envied him. To be out there alone with the shy wild animals and the woodland birds would be the ideal way of watching Nature at work. When out in the woods he told the time by the sun. As a contrast to these real old English ways, at home he owned one of the first gramophones, many years before we had one. The music, Edwardian ditties, squeaked forth from a large trumpet-like horn.

In many places throughout the large area of chestnut copse were to be found these flat, blackened clearings where charcoal was burned at intervals. Doubtless as one cone was burning the charcoal burner would be building up a second one on the same clearing, so that he could stay in his little hut all summer.

Burning charcoal in this primitive manner was on its way out and the use of the end product less in demand. However, thirty years later, during the Second World War, there was a revival, for charcoal was required in gas-masks. Enormous metal drums were then used to make it in. I was still roaming the same woods beloved of childhood days and I remember the disgust I felt at seeing these untidy monstrosities left rusting after the war was over. I am afraid the lines from a hymn have been often called to mind:

> "Though every prospect pleases
> And only man is vile."

I have no wish whatever to go to the moon, but whenever I see her pale orb in the night sky I am saddened to think now of man's debris lying there spoiling her pristine purity.

SPECIAL CORNERS OF OUR WOODS

But back to happy childhood days in our quiet woodlands. Across a couple of fields was a steep slope that in Spring was carpeted with bluebells. Looking down under the trees one saw a blue haze as far as the eye could see. Lifting one's head to the distance there rose Henley Hill and beyond that the South Downs, a range of long rounded humps against the blue sky. Here at the top of the slope Father put a seat which was inevitably known as the *Bluebell Seat*. It was made of chestnut cut just there and it fitted into the landscape perfectly.

I connect this seat particularly with Sundays. Perhaps we came here sometimes on Sunday evenings as a fitting end to a relaxed, leisurely day set apart from the routine of the work-a-day week.

Not content with making a garden full of delightful surprises, and placing a rustic seat at a few strategic points, Father and the boys built the Robbers' Cave. This was no cave but a little fort made of stones picked up round about and built against a steep bank. It is probable that this hollow in the wood was also the remains of a stone quarry. Here we played by the hour, revelling in the romantic name. It was a very secluded spot. No path led to it; one just scrambled up through the trees in the deep leaf-litter as best as one could. We spent much of our time hollowing out the bank behind the ramparts, and patching these up, filling in gaps with tufts of moss.

Now and then we took a picnic there with sausages to cook over a fire of our own making. Big brothers certainly had their uses!

On one disused charcoal burner's site Father also built a log cabin, like a small Canadian settler's home. This again was the focal point for many a picnic and hours of contented play. It was a particularly lovely spot for the chestnut ended there and beyond was a tall pine-wood; I can still see vividly in my mind's-eye the tall orange-brown tree trunks rising high into the sunshine, topped with that bluish foliage so entirely different from our other native trees. We would run under them on the carpet of dry pine-needles and gather pine-cones for our fire. We also found the shredded cores and scattered scales left around a flat tree stump that a squirrel had used as its table. In those days they were all red squirrels, for the American grey squirrel had not yet spread through the country.

Undoubtedly it was those early experiences of woodcraft that made my brothers such exceptionally good scoutmasters in later life. They appreciated the real thing. Jan, when scoutmaster of the Camelsdale Troop, took the boys on long day hikes through these same woods, cooking their meal en route. One day they found a rabbit just killed by a stoat and straightway skinned, gutted and cooked it. George led rover-scouts over the wildest parts of Dartmoor by moonlight, finding by compass Cranmere Pool. Here they wrote a postcard to the Chief Scout Lord Baden-Powell, leaving it in the box there to be collected and posted in a more civilised location by the next brave adventurers over this expanse of trackless bog. Christopher took scouts over the Yorkshire Moors pulling a single-wheeler trek-cart carrying their gear. They camped in a different spot each night and moved on for days on end. Hugh became an expert camp cook and was invaluable as quartermaster to my cub camps, baking in biscuit tins buried under the ashes of a trench fire. This was the kind of life we all enjoyed, inspired by our early play days.

The constant change in the woodland scene caused by the felling of chestnut brought about a variation in the flowers also. Bluebells flowered profusely until the trees became really heavy upon them. Primroses gave up sooner, and were, in any case, much more common down on the clay in the valley where there were oak woods under-planted with hazel. This latter was also cut at intervals, "coppiced" for pea-sticks and faggots. On a newly cleared piece there would be acres of yellow primroses, well out before the stately oaks rising high above them came into leaf.

FLOWER GATHERING

An annual event was for a large party, including our church-going aunts, to pick primroses to decorate Haslemere church for Easter. We picked baskets-full and it seemed to make no difference. Somehow the woods appeared much more floriferous then. Perhaps the coppicing was done more regularly. People thought nothing of taking a few plants back to their gardens. A generation or two earlier it was quite the thing for grand ladies, with baskets and trowels (and, like Mother, surrounded by lots of children), and dig up as many as they liked without a thought that they were robbing the countryside.

Even Elizabeth Fry, wealthy Quaker, prison reformer and "great lover of nature," was not above such sacrilege, as this quotation from "The Story of Quakerism" states:

> "She was very fond of gardening and in her spare time
> gradually filled the extensive grounds of Plashet with wild
> flowers. Her tall, graceful figure, followed by two or three
> little ones carrying trowels and baskets, became a familiar
> sight. Of all flowers she loved the primrose best, and she
> and her 'little gardeners' filled every nook and cranny with
> them."

It is questionable now, quite apart from the ethics, how well wild flowers look amongst their garden counterparts. Polyanthus and other cultivated primulas are now-a-days so much bigger and brighter that the primrose pales before them. In the days of Elizabeth Fry there would be less distinction between garden and wild flowers.

Foxgloves flourished in the clearings. One year there would be leaves only, the next tall spikes of "folk's gloves," pink and gorgeous in the sunshine. We picked up the fallen flowers and put them on our fingers and waggled them at each other. We soon learned not to poke our fingers up the flowers on the stem. An angry buzz and we withdrew hastily.

Along the edges of the paths and in damp ruts trailed several dainty little gems: yellow pimpernel and the less common trailing St John's-wort, lesser skullcap, self-heal and ground ivy; wild forget-me-not, so like our garden plant on a minute scale. I am sure I did not know the names of most of these treasures though my mind, through my eyes, was being trained all through childhood to find them and notice small differences. I remember in early adulthood being ashamed that I knew far fewer names of flowers than of birds, and I hastened to put the matter right. Before that time, when in 1917 I was twelve years old and we moved to Somerset, it was like going to a new country to find so many different plants, for we were then in the limestone area of the Mendips. I was particularly fascinated with the little ferns growing in the walls there and soon learned their names. There is nothing like meeting a contrast to open one's mind more widely.

CHESTNUTS AND BERRIES

Here and there in the woods clumps of sweet chestnut trees had been left to grow big. One such was not far from the Robbers' Cave. They were fine specimens with trunks deeply gnarled in a spiral pattern, and in autumn were laden with nuts. They dropped to the ground in their prickly cases and we would rub them back and forth beneath our boots to break them open so that we could pick out the shiny brown chestnuts. Some years these were quite large enough to be worth gathering to take home and roast in a coal shovel over the sitting-room fire. Woe betide us if we forgot to prick or cut the skin beforehand. Then when hot the nut would explode, scattering fragments all around.

I must jump ahead here to October 1914 to tell the tale of the Belgian refugees. There was an unoccupied house belonging to Father just down the hill, and one day he went up to London to a large hall where refugees from the German occupation of Antwerp sat around waiting to be housed. Father picked out a family and brought them down by train and straightaway in the dark evening, housed them in "The Chalet." That night the wind rose and a storm raged. All night long there was a banging on the roof and next day the poor, frightened townsfolk departed back to London convinced that anywhere was safer than this backwoods place where just anything might happen. But it was only a rain of sweet chestnuts falling, and all that autumn Father organised us to gather in this food for free – barrow-loads of it which was stored in the attic against the unknown rigours of war. One of our staple supper dishes that winter was boiled chestnuts. They needed a lot of preparation and we would sit round the table before the meal peeling them. We were divided in our opinion as to whether it was easier to peel before or after cooking them, but Mother served up some tasty and certainly filling meals for us.

It almost seemed as if "God would provide" (some might even have said God was on our side!) for never before or since have I known such a crop.

Father has had a good innings in this chapter, but Mother has a very practical niche in my memory as the provider of meals and of a certain coercion in her manner to make us help.

Each summer, choosing a hot July day, Mother would muster us, those considered old enough, the lower age limit set at about seven years I guess. We would set off with her in our oldest summer clothes, Mother in a large apron and shady hat, and with our picnic make our way through the woods and up to the top of Blackdown. We had a pause at Cotchet Farm before making the final ascent, to drink from the trough of cold spring water that overflowed into a stream below. We would cool our heated brows, etc, and then to business.

Cotchet Farm in 1877. The open heathland remained
until well into the twentieth century.

Upon Blackdown we set to whortleberry-ing, all day. We children picked into enamel mugs and if and when the mug was filled we emptied it into Mother's basket. The berries were small and it took so long even to cover the bottom of the mug, especially if one indulged one's appetite now and again. The bushes were low and I am sure Mother's back must have ached much more than mine, but she was in deadly earnest. We *needed* them. I cannot speak for my brothers, but I know I often stopped picking and then felt guilty. Not without cause either, for there would be a hint of sarcasm in Mother's voice when she made some such remark as "Well, you aren't getting on much, are you?" Then there would be disaster – an almost full mug would be spilt, and whether it was quicker to try to retrieve the fallen berries from deep in the undergrowth or to start afresh remained an unsolved question.

I ate more than were good for me, and as I always managed to sit on them and get purple stains on my cotton frock, I was in trouble on at least three counts by the end of the day. Whortleberry picnics were not the enjoyment they were intended to be.

Whortleberry is the south of England name for what Northerners call bilberries, though the true country folk of Surrey and Sussex referred to them as Hurts (or 'urrts'). There is a hill, part of Hindhead, called Hurt Hill (or of course if you prefer it 'urt 'ill).

To jump forward again, this time to the Second World War when I was principal of my own little school. I then took the liberty two or three times of taking the children of seven to nine years up to Marley Common to pick whortleberries. Twenty children picking for about half an hour collected quite a basketful and enjoyed it. They enjoyed it twice over for the next day delicious tarts appeared for dinner, cooked by Mother who still retained her feeling for "food for free." What satisfaction the children felt in eating the fruits of their own labour!

After the war we had two Swiss girls as domestics for a year. They were shocked that the local people did not flock to the commons to clear them of every whortleberry. Many evenings they went up to Marley and picked for us, always returning to tell us reproachfully that they hadn't met anyone! The Swiss, though neutral, had suffered considerable food shortage and did not forget it easily.

Now, blackberrying was a different thing altogether. They were bigger and covered the bottom of one's mug much more quickly; and one did not have to stand on one's head to get them. There was great competition between us children to see who could fill their mug the most times. "I've covered the bottom of my mug" someone would call out. "Mine's half-full," another would retort. Sometimes we would stick to the rule we applied to raspberry picking: Eat one in ten, no more. At other times we would see how long we could survive without eating any at all. We scrambled about the bushes along the hedgerows, using a walking-stick to pull down the high sprays. Pricks and scratches went unnoticed, and of course the ultimate reward came with all the tasty uses the blackberries were put to – blackberry and apple pies and puddings during the season, jam and jelly to fill the pantry shelves for the rest of the year. There is no flavour to equal pure blackberry jelly without the addition of apple. A favourite cold sweet which I do not think I should enjoy much now was "Summer

Pudding." This was, of course, long before the time of ice-cream in the home, and most puddings were either baked or boiled. This one was not cooked, at least not after the fruit had been stewed with sugar. A large pudding basin was lined with slices of white bread. Into this was poured the stewed fruit, generally black-currants, raspberries, or blackberries. More bread slices were placed on top then a plate and a weight to keep it pressed down. Left overnight the juice penetrated the bread and the whole could be turned out on to a dish for dinner the next day. This was considered a great treat only slightly spoilt if bits of white bread still showed. I fear I was rather a fussy little eater!

With a large and growing family to feed on a slender budget Mother became very canny and resourceful, wasting nothing and never counting the time taken on fruit picking, sorting, "topping and tailing" (gooseberries), "stringing" (currants) and preserving. It was to stand her in good stead in two world wars through which she steered the household with devotion.

Well, here we are, home again from the woods and surrounding country. But we were to wander further still as legs grew longer and stronger.

IN THE WOODS

A view from Blackdown in 1936

FURTHER AFIELD

"Across the high hills and the sea,
And all the changeful skies."

Rudyard Kipling

The holiday at Whitecliffe Bay with Grandfather Hutchinson and Grandmother Woods. This precious old photograph shows signs of wear.

FURTHER AFIELD

THE GREENHILL

Moses Hill ended in a spur just beyond our house and then dropped precipitously for several hundred yards before sloping more gently to Fernhurst in the bottom of the valley.

There was no definite path down this precipice, but under the beech trees that grew all the way down, the earth was more or less bare and we slithered down as best as we could, clutching at a branch here and there and trying not to get into a run from which it would be impossible to stop. I once, years later, saw a child do just this. She ran till she fell and rolled down and down. Hurrying after her as fast as I safely could I was prepared to find her with every bone broken but she picked herself up completely unhurt. Such is the resilience of childhood.

This slope was the quickest(!) way to the best primrose woods and through them to the Greenhill, associated in my literal mind with the hymn, "There is a green hill far away," though I wondered why anyone supposed it should have had a city wall.

It was a hillock completely covered in large beech trees. Some people called it Beechen Tod and others, very aptly, the Cathedral Wood. Instinctively one entered it quietly, almost reverently, feeling dwarfed beneath the tall, stately grey tree-trunks topped in spring by the softest green foliage, and aflame in autumn with coppery leaves that drifted down one by one to settle slowly on the leaf-carpeted floor. But our reverence soon turned to joyous merriment as we scuffed through the dead leaves and took a running jump into the saw-pit. This was a trench some ten feet long and originally six feet deep; now it was half-filled with a soft bed of leaves. It had been used to cut tree trunks into planks long before circular saws and other mechanical devices had been invented. The saw used was a two-handed rip-saw. We had one hanging up in our barn and I often watched two men sawing logs, one at either end, pushing and pulling.

Here in the wood a tree trunk was laid along the length of the trench. One man stood on top and the other in the trench and by pushing and pulling the saw vertically up and down they sawed the trunk into planks. The man on top had the hardest work, but the one beneath got covered with saw-dust. I recently watched a demonstration of this at the Weald and Downland Open-Air Museum at Singleton in Sussex. It looked incredibly hard work.

But what fun it was to us children to see how far we could jump into the saw-pit. And when in we would scatter leaves over each other much as children in the sea splash each other.

The leaves had all blown off the crown of this hillock leaving bare, dry earth with here and there strange and beautiful toadstools and cushions of pale green moss that I know now as *Leucobrijum glaucum.* It was partial to that kind of situation, and being dry easily came adrift and rolled down the hill. Though our way through the woods to the Greenhill was flowery indeed, under the beeches none grew. It was too shady.

Many years later the beeches were all felled and the whole area planted with conifers. I suspect the beeches had passed their optimum and were dying anyway, but it seemed such sacrilege that I had no heart to go there any more.

RAMBLES AND DISCOVERIES

Another ramble Father liked to take us on was into the woods below Fernhurst called Minepit Copse. Here we visited the ruins of buildings around and over a pretty stream that had once been an iron-foundry. I never understood how this worked, but was shown the rusty red clay, and the same coloured sediment in the stream. Somehow this was converted by burning much oak wood in a kiln to make cannon for the Battle of Trafalgar and the railings around St Paul's Cathedral. I was suitably impressed, so much so that when the said railings were removed during the Second World War to convert into armaments I said to myself "There go our railings."

I tried to listen to Father's explanations, but was glad when they were over and I could paddle in the cool stream. One day we found a rat sitting on a stone in the stream. Funny that, with all our noise and chatter it did not go away. We went right up to it. It was stone dead!

Mother led us to Blackdown to pick whortleberries. Father took us there to look for flints. There was one particular spot, the edge of a sandy track near the dew-pond that had been a flint-knappers "factory". A great many very small flints were found there and although it had been excavated we still found pieces. Nearby also were some small depressions in the ground that we were told were the remains of pit dwellings of Stone-Age man. Whether the ponds called "mist ponds" were purely natural or were also dug by these men is a matter of conjecture, but without them there would be no water on this hill, the highest in the district.

A 'Mist Pond' on Blackdown circa 1905

We would paddle in these clear pools and look for the strange plant that 'ate' insects in its leaves – sundew. The moss there was so different from the dry little hummocks we found at the Greenhill. It was bog-moss, soft and spongy. One could pick up a handful and squeeze out the water. In very dry weather bog-moss shrivelled almost to nothing, but swelled up and went on growing as soon as it became wet again.

Damsel-flies, those dainty little blue and black or red and black striped dragonflies whizzed about. They were much smaller than the handsome great yellow ones that we disturbed when we played in the pond at home.

We went as near as we could to the house, Aldworth, where the great poet Lord Tennyson had lived and died, but it was all very private, and it was not until many years later that I was able to visit the house built on the ledge looking down over the Weald of Sussex to Chanctonbury Ring and beyond.

On a sunny morning one could see a silver line of sea shining through a gap in the Downs which we early learnt to call The Amberley Gap. Tennyson referred to the view as "Green Sussex fading into blue with one grey line of sea."

Father was a devotee of Tennyson's poems and would read them to us. Sadly I never learnt to appreciate poetry except for a few pleasant, simple pieces describing my beloved countryside. But I was duly impressed by pictures of this great man in his cloak and large black hat, and basked in the reflected glory of the fact that Mother and Father had actually seen him on Haslemere Station. When he lay dying Uncle Roger took his wife, Aunt Eleanor, who had been a nurse, to stay with him while he went to the station to meet the London doctor and take him to the Poet Laureate's bedside. This was in 1892, some twelve years before I was born.

Like Moses Hill, Blackdown ended in a spur at the southern tip. This was called the "Temple of the Winds." Whether Tennyson gave it this name or not I do not know, but it was very fitting. There was a clump of Scots pines through which the wind forever blew, and the view was very similar to that from Aldworth.

I must be permitted here to tell of the midnight walk we children made to the Temple of the Winds when we were grown up. It was New Year's Eve, a lovely dry night, and we made our way by moonlight all the way up through the woods and over the common and stood there listening to the church bells of many little villages away in the valley below us. They rang in the New Year from Lurgashall and Lodsworth, Northchapel and possibly as far off as Petworth, Plaistow and Tillington. Quaint country names these, of peaceful villages scattered among the fields and forests of one of our most cherished counties, Sussex by the sea.

The children of each generation take for granted their circumstances and way of life, particularly if their parents appear to do so. We were brought up in the knowledge that what money we had must be spent sparingly and always on worthwhile things. Thus we never had fireworks though we made a huge bonfire and burnt Guy Fawkes, also of our own making, with great excitement. We were early taught that whatever is most worth having in life is that for which we have striven.

This applied equally to excursions and holidays. They were indeed hard-won. At the time I think most of us were proud of our walking ability, though thinking back I wonder if we did not overdo this exercise.

If only Father did not walk so fast! He was tall, spare and long-legged. He quite forgot that inevitably we had to take many more strides than he did and sometimes we were very, very tired and foot-sore. It was soon forgotten however.

NYEWOOD BRICKWORKS

An all-day excursion would be taken now and again to the Nyewood Brickworks some ten miles away. We would totter down the steep slope off the end of Moses Hill again, and down the incredibly muddy track on Van Common. Here there were several quaint old cottages. This took us to Chapel Street in Fernhurst which we crossed and made our way by footpaths through Minepit Copse and Lords Common, on and on, I know not the actual route, till we came at last to the village of Rogate. Here we passed a fine old church and I cannot think we passed it without sometimes going in, for old churches were another of Father's passions. It was cool inside if the day was hot, but often it was too cool and I would have preferred to stay outside in the sunshine.

Now it was only about a mile further on. We crossed the River Rother, a bigger stream than any we had near home, by a fine old stone bridge and just beyond was a colony of sand martins nesting in a sandy bank that must at some have time been a quarry, it was so high. We might pause a few minutes to watch the parent birds fly in to feed their young that peeped out of their nesting holes.

We would soon be urged on again and it was now not more than half a mile to our destination.

Probably we had rested somewhere en route and eaten our sandwiches, unless they were partaken now. Anyway all trace of fatigue vanished in the interest of watching the bricks and tiles being made by hand.

There was a certain amount of machinery for I remember a constant flow of pugged clay moving along a wooden trough the width and depth of a brick. As it reached a certain point it was cut off by wires (as cheese was cut in the grocer's shop) and then each brick was put into a mould and finished off by hand.

The men working there were friendly and let me make my own brick and tile on which I would scratch my initials with a stick. Then I dusted it over with a little sand in the approved manner. Doubtless after we had gone my efforts were returned to the pugging machine.

I have vague memories of pugging being done by hand, clay with a certain quantity of sand being churned about in a large barrel by a man with a heavy wooden club, till it was of the right consistency. Whether this is correct I am not sure, for the records of improvements made by Father when he bought the Brickfield include pugging by machinery. Another improvement was the moving of the brickfield to a new site against the railway station where a special siding was made for loading the bricks.

They were very colourful bricks and tiles, a warm red, and were popular not only locally but for export. Many found their way to America, and Central Europe. Bricklayers employed by Father were building a nobleman's palace in Luxembourg when the 1914 War broke out and they had to hurry home. It was due to the war that the Nyewood Brickfield lost the contract to supply bricks for the Crown Prince's new palace at Potsdam. In fact the war put an end to Father's ownership of this enterprising business.

Though much of this knowledge I gleaned in later years I was well aware of the importance of the siding when we saw trucks laden ready to be taken away. A whole trainload was destined for America.

After business was over we would go to the Manager's house beside the old brickyard where his wife, kind Mrs English, gave us tea. There were plates of fresh bread and butter, lashings of home-made jam and fruit cake. This was served on a lacey tablecloth in her sitting-room full of knick-knacks and those diverse ornaments so beloved of the Victorian front room.

The old brickyard was overgrown with scrub: willow and bramble, hazel and that delectable shrub found here and there in the woods, guelder-rose. In autumn its leaves turned brilliant red and clusters of glistening berries hung like redcurrants. It was here that I heard my first nightingale. One never forgets a "life-bird" or the spot where it was located.

Home again. This time by train to Petersfield where we changed onto the main Portsmouth to London train, dropping off at Haslemere Station. And here came the rub! Every excursion, however long, always ended with that two mile trudge up to Moses Hill.

Never mind. We were healthy youngsters. There was a warm glow on our faces (if a few blisters on our heels); and settling cosily around the fire we had much to tell Mother of our day's adventures.

SEA-SIDE HOLIDAYS

I do not think a sea-side holiday was quite an annual event, though more than once a kind aunt, twice at least Aunt Elsie Newman, paid for a holiday for us. This must have been quite an item for a family growing as ours was, though of course we did not go to hotels.

The Isle of Wight was our usual venue, and was within easy reach by train and boat, as it is still. My very first remembrance of anything at all was when I was two years and eight months. It is quite an isolated incident. I was rolling in the sand at the edge of the sea and getting covered in sand, then rolling in the water and washing it off again. I did this again and again while big brother George splashed me and we laughed together. There was a special pleasure in being allowed to get all dirty as I thought without being scolded.

This incident took place at Whitecliff Bay and we were staying in the house above the bay that later became a boys' school. Grandfather had taken the house and sent down four families, the Allen Chandlers, Roger Hutchinsons, the Roshers, (Evelyn, and the triplets who were only two years old) and ourselves. Several unmarried aunts came to help. I hope they enjoyed it! A photograph shows how Aunt Kitty drilled all of us who would be so coerced. We are standing to attention and saluting. What, I wonder? The Trips were too young so I am the smallest there, standing in the front saluting with the best. It is just as well that no photograph was taken of Mother hauling me up the steep path from the beach for I am told I was a hefty weight; nor of course of me stealing the Trips' biscuits at night. I was reminded of these troubles much later. My recollections of sea-side holidays do not run in any chronological order, but that is not of any real significance.

THE PARAPHERNALIA OF BATHING

Much has been written in biographies about children of the late Victorian and Georgian eras bathing from bathing machines, being ducked by brawny and brutal bathing women and though I do not remember these horrors, we certainly used bathing machines. These were drawn down to the water's edge. Then, very discreetly because the said machine was packed with female relatives, all with their backs to each other, we got into our bathing costumes. We gingerly descended the steps getting colder and colder as we became gradually immersed.

Bathing costumes were more like combinations, complete with short sleeves, buttons down the front to the waist, and the whole reaching the knees. Hugh and I each had a costume of stockinette in red and white rings. I must say we looked rather sweet. I remember the photograph that shows this, for I was bravely sitting in two inches of water but Hugh had refused even to do that. So he stands holding my hand and beaming disarmingly.

Mother's costume I shall never forget! It was made of pink

flannelette and was voluminous. As she walked down into the water and it gradually got wet from the bottom upwards, air that was trapped inside was pushed up and made the dry part blow out like a balloon. As the costume had seen years of spasmodic use and was faded, the wet part became redder showing up the faded pink more and more. It was not until Mother had taken the plunge completely that one ceased to feel embarrassed. She could swim a little and tried to teach us, not with much success I fear. Kit was soon blue with cold and retired to the men's bathing machine to dress again. All I wanted to do was splash about in the edge where it was comparatively warm, and SAFE.

I must say we looked rather sweet (and brave) in two inches of water

Bathing machines cost money and on one holiday Mother, always "careful", decided we would dispense with one. We repaired to a quiet bay with many rocks behind which we could hide to undress, but it was supposed to be private. Our bathe therefore, was to be quiet and unobtrusive. Alas, away from the flat sandy beach I was used to I suddenly found myself up to the armpits in water. I let out an almighty yell and had to be hastily rescued. And Mother tried to hush me up but I was not to be silenced so easily. We were all called in and dressed and retreated ignominiously. I was given to understand in no uncertain terms that it was all my fault.

SEA-SIDE ACTIVITIES

Sand castles, little cottages decorated with sea-shells and different coloured sea-weeds, paddling in rock pools etc, etc, all the things normal children go to the sea-side for were entirely enjoyable. What was *not* my idea was the daily service held by some mission which we were encouraged to attend and which some of my older brothers actually enjoyed. I would linger on the edge of the crowd and slip away when I had had enough. We seemed to be endlessly singing

> "I am H-A-P-P-Y
> I am H-A-P-P-Y
> I know I am, I know I am,
> I am H-A-P-P-Y."

"Culture" on the sands at Sandown. Father reading history to a rather bored audience (I had escaped and George is about to do so)

Nor did I consider it to be in context for Father to read History to us. We nestled under the esplanade out of the wind, filtering the dry sand through our fingers idly and hoped it would end soon. Apparently not one of the older boys dared to say anything, but on some occasion when Father had us thus in his grip I piped up boldly, "That's enough Father, I want to go and play." I do not remember this myself, but Mother chuckled over it years later.

Picnics on the sea-shore too could be rather a trial. Sandwiches, the very word describes what we were eating. If the wind had not already blown sand onto them our hands were sticky with salty sand, and not infrequently an eatable got dropped. Rugs spread out for us to sit on got crumpled up and sandy, and the more we complained and squealed the more we were scolded for not being more careful. I imagine the whole holiday was quite hard work and frustrating for our parents.

We were not interested in the donkey rides, there was *Zephyr* at home, but along the esplanade of, I think, Sandown, there were goat-carriages. These were for very little children and Hugh and Mary sat prettily in a little carriage, Mary having snatched the reins, as they were led along by a boy.

What we enjoyed quite as much as the seasideness of our holidays was the exploration of the strange landslip country near Ventnor. Huge chunks of land had fallen from the cliff to make an under-cliff of woodland and scrub over an area of perhaps half a mile wide and two or three miles long. Through it wandered small paths making their way round great boulders. It was a glorious place to play robbers or hide-and-seek and we had a favourite hummock that was flat on top and mossy, where one could picnic in comfort. Someone had left tomato skins about! Tomatoes were not all that common in those days. We examined them with interest.

Inland from the undercliff rose white cliffs, draped in ivy and old-mans-beard. There were steps up to the top and then a path along the edge, in some places so near that one had to be careful not to dislodge the earth and fall down.

A FIRST AEROPLANE

The highest Down above Ventnor was St Boniface. One day a fete was held up there, the chief attraction of which was a real "live" aeroplane. Mother was our leader on this occasion. She it was who seemed more readily to grasp the historic, epoch- making, events of the day and made sure her children witnessed them. So we clambered up the steep, slippery grass to the top and there it was! We foregathered with the crowd as this marvellous invention, the bi-plane, revved up and took off right over our heads. It was a breath-taking moment as the machine glided off the Down and made out to sea.

Jan with a huge grin on his face declared he had touched it as it passed over. I wonder.

This was in 1911, only two years after M. Bleriot had made the first flight from France to England in his flying machine.

The pilot of the plane at Ventnor was one Valentine. Whether he was taking people up for rides I am not sure, but he must have been quite one of the first that the public had an opportunity of seeing.

Not long after this Hugh remembers that a balloon came over Moses Hill. We all rushed out to see it and Hugh suddenly realised he was clutching his plate and spoon. It was pudding time and he was on his way from the nursery to the kitchen to "ask for more."

RECOLLECTIONS OF TRAVEL

Talking of hard-won holidays, all through our childhood travelling was done in the most economical way, often part-way by bicycle or on our own two feet. It was a couple of years after we had left our hill-top, but were still at Kingsley Green that Hugh and I did our marathon.

Father took us to Ventnor, but the manner of our going was certainly spartan. Hugh was about eight and a half and I was three years older. We walked to Midhurst, six miles. That was nothing. From there we took the train to Portsmouth via Petersfield, and the boat across to Ryde, a lovely interlude. We then – wait for it – walked right across the Isle of Wight, fourteen miles.

At Shanklin we found the Roshers playing on the beach. Hugh and I took off our boots and stockings and cooled our tired feet by paddling the length of the bay as we chatted with our cousins.

Eventually we reached Ventnor in the early evening where we set to, to look for lodgings for the rest of the family who were coming down the next day. We found these in two houses nearby. Landladies were generally kind and homely and we had a good holiday after our strenuous beginning.

Our near neighbour Mrs Matthay (second from the left)
with Myra Hess (standing) and Bertel on Zephyr

FRIENDS AND NEIGHBOURS

"This happy breed of men, this little world."

William Shakespeare

The main road through Kingsley Green.
(L) The Old Bakery; (R) Miss Tateham Jones' House

FRIENDS AND NEIGHBOURS

THE SHOP AT KINGSLEY GREEN

When we first moved to Moses Hill it was the only house up there. Life must have seemed somewhat restricted for Mother without any near neighbours, but she was busy managing her own domain and her domestic life would have been too full for much sociability in any case.

It was not far to drop down to the cluster of houses, cottages and shop that constituted the hamlet of Kingsley Green. A row of buildings joined together consisted of a couple of cottages, the bakery and shop where Mr and Mrs Ebenezer Mills lived, and the Toll House right against the main road. Though very old, this was not the actual Toll House; that had been on the other side of the main road and was no longer in existence.

Mrs Mills was keeping pace with Mother in having boy babies just before my time and Nurse Castle attended her confinements also. She stopped at four boys, but as we know, Mother was not half way through her family.

Across the main road were two more very old houses, and later on several others were built up what was called Hatch Lane. Down the main road towards Haslemere stood another bakery owned by cousins of Ebenezer Mills. This was a charming old house set back in its cottage garden. Sadly, years later, it was demolished to widen the road. The baking there had long since stopped and "Eb" had the monopoly.

What workers these Mills's were! The shop stocked everything from candles to clothes pegs, paraffin to potatoes. There were large jars of boiled sweets in the window and one could buy two bulls-eyes for a farthing. Behind the counter, on a dresser, stood huge slabs of butter and cheese off which pounds and half-pounds were accurately cut with a wire. Home-cooked ham was there, and on the floor sacks of sugar and flour. A scoop of a size to hold about a pound shovelled out the contents into stiff blue paper bags standing erect on the scales. Tea was kept in big tins with the name of the brand in fancy scrolled lettering on the outside. One that remains in my memory was "Mazawatee."

Most eatables were weighed out to order, making the grocer's work hard indeed. The scales were used for everything just as they came along and the standard of hygiene was not over fussy. One or two cats were always present, generally asleep on the counter over which passed everything. Cats were an essential part of the ménage for at night mice could have a right royal time.

There was no heating in the shop and with the door continually opening with a ping of the bell attached to it to let customers in or out, it was very cold indeed. At one end of the counter was an oil table lamp kept burning low. Now and then the grocer would warm his hands over it.

There being nothing by way of a church or village hall at Kingsley Green, not even a pub, the shop became the focal point. As a child at Moses Hill I remember nothing of this, but the camaraderie, the hilarity, the pathos, the general exchange of news and views that took place in that crowded little shop during the Second World War would fill a book. Harold, Eb Mills' second son, was in charge then and won all our regard and affection for his fairness and expertise in dealing with ration books, points coupons and the rest. Moreover he was *the* telephone, often used if others were out of service for any reason, and I shall never forget soon after the War ended seeing Harold rush out of the shop leaving a cluster of us waiting, and in at The Toll House as if he was mad. News had come through that the son of that house was safe and on his way home, having been missing in Japanese hands for four years. After that digression we will retrace our steps to the gentler days of the first decade of the twentieth century.

Our bread came hot from the oven just behind the shop, its delicious smell merging with all the others in and around. Here also rich, lardy scones and fruit cakes were baked on Saturdays ready for Sunday teas. Hot-cross buns were baked in the very early hours of Good Friday and delivered to our door in time for breakfast. It was the only day in the year that they were available.

Baking was done in the old-fashioned way and Mills must have been one of the last to carry on this custom, for it continued into the 1950s.

There was an oven in the wall some six feet long. Into this was placed a faggot that fitted it. It was set alight and the iron door closed tight. Outside, in the yard, was an enormous stack of faggots bought from the wood-cutters working in the surrounding copses. They were bundles of twiggy wood, mostly hazel, old and dry enough to burn readily. Each faggot was secured with a piece of hazel that had been twisted while still green.

While the faggot was burning inside the brick oven, "Old Eb" would mix the dough in large wooden troughs, knead it again into large lumps, and, weighing each piece as he pulled it off, shape the loaves. There were cottage loaves with a little loaf on top of a larger base, deliciously crusty, and tin loaves that were baked in individual tins but rose over the top to a brown crust.

When the faggot had burnt itself out the ash was quickly raked away and the bread put in and the door closed again. The baker knew by experience just how long the bread would take to cook and at the same time for the oven to cool.

Mills' bread was delivered all over a wide area by horse and cart.

DAILY DELIVERIES

We did not fetch our bread or most of the groceries. A roundsman called, took the grocery order at the back door and returned with the goods later in the day. Butcher's meat came from Haslemere by the same process. There were regular calling days for these tradesmen and Mother was ready with her list written in a notebook with stiff covers with the name of the shop printed on the front.

Milk, until we had our own, was delivered twice a day fresh and warm from the cow. (What a shame it was that I never liked milk!) It came in churns and the milkman had quart, pint and gill measures which he dipped in and emptied into one's jug. The gill was used generally for measuring cream.

Mills had a small farm around an incredibly old barn which always looked as if the next wind would blow it over, and for years milk was supplied from here to the neighbourhood.

Letters were delivered twice a day by a walking or cycling postman, and there really was a penny post with a bright red stamp. Better still was the postcard which was often used and cost a green halfpenny stamp. There being no telephone Mother would give the postman a postcard to take away in the morning inviting Aunt Kitty to tea the next day. She would get it by the afternoon post and send her reply for Mother to receive the following morning.

In towns there were at least three deliveries daily.

So, although we were perched up on our hill-top we were exceedingly well served by cheerful, friendly tradesmen whom we got to know well, for they stayed in their jobs for years.

There was much whistling and singing as the men went about their work, be it as delivery men, road-menders or farm workers. In this way we picked up the tunes at least of many of the current "pop" music. There being no "mass media" as we know it now, this was the only way we could have learnt them.

No refuse disposal vans of any kind came around our countryside. We disposed of our own refuse by burning or burying. As very few commodities came in tins or bottles (and most bottles would be returnable anyway), this was not difficult. All vegetable waste was either boiled down for the pigs or put on the rubbish heap. The word "compost" came in a little later, I think.

THE TOLL HOUSE TWINS

The Toll House adjoining the shop housed a family we knew for there were twin boys about the same age as myself; lively youngsters. Father was not too keen on our friendship, but surely the young must learn to mix with all sorts and learn by experience and by their faults how to grow up. Situated as we were, a large family in isolation on our hill it was all too easy to become too self-contained, self-satisfied and unadaptable.

There is no doubt that I got into more scrapes with the twins than with my brothers, and they certainly added spice to life. On one occasion when several of our cousins were with us too we formed two gangs, one to storm a hill fortress (where now Otara Nursing Home stands) defended by the other. There was no real animosity in it but we became very rough and resorted to throwing stones which we knew was strictly forbidden. A stone came flying down and hit me on the head making a nasty graze.

I would not tell Mother how it happened and after a day or so she took me to see Grandfather Jonathan Hutchinson, a leading skin specialist. She feared ringworm at least. Still I did not confess, but Grandfather put her mind at rest. It was nothing serious and would soon heal, which of course, it did.

I do not know just how wild and naughty I was becoming but there came a day when Father put his foot down. Two books that the twins had lent me were confiscated and deposited in the bottom drawer under Mother's wardrobe. They were deemed *unsuitable*. I was wasting my time in frivolous living, etc, etc. The maddening thing was that I had not bothered to open those books and do not know to this day the awful extent of their depravity.

After that I saw less of these lively boys and as they presently moved away we lost contact altogether.

EARLY SCHOOLING

For a while I was sent daily down the hill to a governess living at Kingsley Green. She was an elderly lady who led us (there seemed to be several, but I have no recollection of who the others were) in a cracked voice in the singing of French songs such as "Frère Jacques" and "Sur le pont d'Avignon." My impression of lessons all through childhood (until I went to Sidcot School at the age of twelve), is of a hazy feeling of wasted time that would have been better spent out in the sunshine. I did not read fluently till I was eight years old and seldom read a book through before the age of twelve. I remember in my first year at Sidcot being horrified at being expected to read to myself several chapters of *Ivanhoe* for prep. It seemed an impossible task. Now, if it had been a Nature book that would help me to learn more, it would have been an easy matter. The chief thing I remember about Miss Tateham-Jones' class was getting there. I went alone, a walk of perhaps ten minutes. Down the Hollow onto the road that led past the shop, across the main road (no difficulty there) and into her charming little garden. Charming it certainly was for it was tended by her friend who shared the house, Miss Maldon, who was a trained gardener. Looking back, I would think in 1910 there were not many trained lady gardeners, and I wonder if she knew Miss Gertrude Jekyll who lived near Godalming, not more than about ten miles away. The wicket gate through the hedge opened onto the path leading to the front door and either side flower-beds overflowed with colour. The porch and the walls were covered in creepers, shrubs and climbing roses, almost dwarfing the pretty little house.

I wished I knew Miss Maldon better; she was dressed in useful tweedy outdoor skirt and jumper and was busy about things that I would like to have shared in. But in I had to go and stick my nose into books for a couple of hours.

I enjoyed my walk alone down to my lessons until one day I saw a runaway horse. It was on a small side road, later known as Snipe Lane, near Mills' old barn, and was harnessed to a farm cart. It was rearing up and almost tipping the cart over backwards while a man, tugging at the reins tried to control it. He was shouting and doubtless swearing, but the horse made off and he had to let go. Round the corner it careered across the Green and up Marley Lane, the poor man in hot pursuit. It was never very near me, but I scuttled under the fence into a field and made for home as fast as my legs would carry me. Nothing would induce me to go down the hill again that day, though Mother with her usual calm told me I was a little goose, or words to that effect. For long after that I kept inside the field, rather than walk along the road in case a run-away horse came again.

The house, "Kingsley Dene," had been built by Father at the bottom of the Hollow as a private hotel. It was a beautiful house standing a little above the road and commanding a fine view across its lawn to Henley Hill. It was here that I had been such a shy little idiot when asked out to tea. Though I think it never "did" very well financially, and changed hands several times, some interesting people stayed there, including Kenneth Grahame, author of *The Wind in the Willows*. One day Christopher and I were walking home past "Kingsley Dene" in company with Miss Tateham-Jones and Miss Maldon. As they turned in to visit at "Kingsley Dene" we said good-bye and I added "goodriddancetobadrubbish." There was a shocked silence. I can see Miss Jones' face now, lowered, looking at me over the top of her glasses, too pained to speak. Kit shuffled his feet, undecided whether to laugh or scold, or run away. But what had I done? I didn't know. Miss Mathew always said "Goodbye Margaret, goodriddancetobadrubbish." It was just something to say on parting.

We crept away crestfallen, Kit thoroughly ashamed of his sister and I at last realising that grown-ups said with impunity to children what children might never say back. A strange world, but there it was!

We had not been long on our hill before a few houses were built and this southern end of Marley became known as Marley Heights.

TOBIAS MATTHAY ARRIVES

The first was designed by Father for Professor Matthay on the very tip of the hill, and it commanded one of the finest views in West Sussex. Up in the attic there was a telescope through which we were invited to look right away to the sea through the Amberley Gap. I took it on trust that it was indeed the sea. It was just a faint line on the horizon.

Tobias Matthay was a well-known teacher of the piano. He himself had studied under Sterndale Bennett and Sir Arthur Sullivan. He became famous for perfecting a particularly flowing and pleasant touch on the instrument and published a book called *The Art of Touch*. His approach was generally known as The Matthay Method. There were only a couple of fields between our house and High Marley across which sounds of music floated. Of course, most of his teaching took place in London, but many pupils came down to stay and Myra Hess, probably Matthay's most famous pupil, was a frequent visitor. We boasted that she once played on our piano. Mother became very friendly with Mrs Matthay whom I remember as a warm, kindly person, rather large, dressed in loose artistic dresses of the period and with hair worn in a plait round the head. She was sister to Mrs Kennedy Frazer who collected and made famous the Hebridean Songs. Much later we had a record of some of these lovely, lilting melodies. So Mother knew her also and her daughter Patoufa, or Toufa for short. A strange name easy to remember.

Tobias Matthay was a rather small man with very thick glasses. We were shy of him. He probably had little use for a rabble of country children as he had none of his own, but each Christmas we attended a sumptuous party at their house. Though I remember little about these I fear they were somewhat marred as usual by each child being expected to "say something" or sing something. This was a most tiresome habit of grown-ups against which modern children would rebel successfully. My rebelliousness never got very far in those days.

The Matthays were the first on our hill to own a car. It was driven by a Frenchman who lived with them in some capacity or other. What insular, conservative brats we were! We laughed to scorn his curious English and also at the car, seeing no future in either. So it was on one of the occasions when I was under the influence of the twins that we lay in wait at the top of a high bank as the car chugged slowly up the hill, and dropped a stone neatly on its bonnet. Monsieur stopped, got out, examined the car, looked around, saw nothing, got in and continued chugging on.

When war broke out in 1914 there was considerable mistrust of the foreigners in our midst and of people with unusual names, and suspicion fell on innocent Tobias Matthay. One warm summer evening he was strolling on his lawn in contemplative fashion when he found himself surrounded by soldiers creeping from the rhododendrons. He was led into the house where questions were asked and he was requested to remove the telescope. Nothing more happened but poor "Uncle Tobs" was most upset.

He was not *altogether* and always above reproach however, for years later, again in the gloaming, I came across the old gentleman trying to top some fir trees on Father's land with a long pruning hook. He peered at me through his thick lenses and pretended to be doing nothing in particular, so I pretended likewise. After all, what did it matter? The trees were so tall one could hardly see their tops and if they were spoiling that view of the sea, well, good luck to him! Certainly it was not worth incurring Father's wrath. But, I wonder?

The Second World War was about to start.

MY PIANO LESSONS

It is unfortunate that, living so near a great Modern teacher of music Mother should be persuaded into having me taught the piano in the old-fashioned thumping way.

A dear little old lady called Mrs Hecht, also of foreign extraction, built a house called "Open Combe," and lived there with her daughter, Mrs Morris. There was a pleasant, tweedy, bearded Mr Morris also but I rather fancy his wife, metaphorically speaking, wore the trousers. Anyway these two ladies also became friendly with Mother and Mrs M. undertook to start me on the dreary path of musicianship. All she succeeded in doing, however, was to set me against it, for her personality was not one to inspire love, admiration or anything else pleasant in a small girl. She patronised. She gushed. She suffocated me with misplaced affection. "Margaret," she simpered one day, "do you know why we call you the chicken? It is because you are the youngest person who comes to our house." Chicken indeed! I suppose, with hindsight, I ought to be forgiving, but this story is about how I felt then. Nothing but dislike, to put it mildly.

We sat close together at the piano to play simple duets, lifting hands high and crashing down on any notes they happened on. The noise was dreadful. I am not musical but pleasant sounds please me, others definitely offend.

I begged Mother to release me from this torture, but she said it was so kind of Mrs Morris. I fancy she felt sorry for her childless condition so I became a sort of sacrificial offering.

It was a vegetarian household and to our dismay Mother picked up some of their cranky recipes. One consisted of a mess of porridge oats and dried fruit and what-not boiled in a cloth and served in the name of pudding. Such recipes did not bear repetition at our dinner table.

One awful day I was invited there to dinner and was fed elderberry blancmange. It tasted of ink, and although I piled on sugar again and again it was the hardest thing to swallow.

There came an unusually warm day in early May and Father and Mother had gone abroad for a holiday. We children were in the care of Phoebe and a maid. In my comfortable blue serge frock I walked up the hill (for we had recently left Moses Hill) for my music lesson and arrived evidently looking rather hot. With exclamations about my state and the fact that my dear Mother was away Mrs M. sat me at the piano to practise while she set to and shortened a dress of her own for me.

It was what was known as a jibbah; a loose affair with wide magyar sleeves, dark grey with lighter grey yoke and coarse black embroidery round the neck. The sort a lady friend of Bunthorne might have worn in the greenery-yallery days.

For hours it seemed I thumped away at the piano and Mrs M., mouth full of pins, gave advice while stitching at the hem. Then I was made to take off my frock (undress in front of her!) and put the ugly thing on.

Oh the shame of it all! I left the house and, fearful of being seen by anyone, made my way home by a circuitous route through the woods. Phoebe was on her knees spring-cleaning the nursery. "There!" I said, "You can clean the floor with that!" And I tore it off and flung it down among the soapsuds.

Phoebe was as incensed as I was. Was she not in charge in my parents' absence? What an interfering old so-and-so that Mrs M. was. *Ne'er cast a clout till May be out, etc, etc.* We had a good hate meeting together as I got into my beloved old serge again and felt better.

THE HOULDERS AT SPUR POINT

Completely different were our third neighbours Mr and Mrs Houlder at "Spur Point." The name exactly described the position of this fine house. Mr Houlder was a retired director of the Shipping Line of that name. A big, smart gentleman who looked his best mounted on his chestnut hunter. His little wife was a gentle lady, slightly lame. She kept a beautifully furnished home and gave elegant tea-parties. I was not averse to going to these with Mother, for the atmosphere was relaxed and somehow geared to making children feel quietly content. Little scones and cakes, wafer thin bread and butter on lacey doilies and brought in by a maid in starched apron and cap somehow was not too daunting, and this must have been due to the genuine kindness and ease of our host and hostess.

After tea Mr Houlder would regale us with songs. Standing by the piano as his wife played the accompaniments, he was indeed the dashing Victorian gentleman.

One song remains in my memory. It struck me at the time as being extremely humorous:

> Is your Mother in, Mollie Malone?
> Mollie said "She's out."
> Is your father in, Mollie Malone?
> Mollie smiled "He's out."

> Then may I come in by the fire-side,
> And sit with you awhile?
> Mollie said with a sigh,
> "You can't do that
> For the fire's out too."

Mr Houlder on his hunter was all very fine, but my dismay was great indeed when one day he persuaded me up on to its back myself. It seemed an incredible height. I was led slowly round the paddock, clinging on with all my might till I was lifted down again. As I never ever mounted *Zephyr,* our donkey, who in their senses could imagine I would tolerate a great big horse!

Over the coach-house at Spur Point lived the coachman with his wife and little girl. She was about my age and we enjoyed playing together sometimes. She at least did not lead me into mischief and I hope I did her no moral harm either.

A RETIRED HEAD-MISTRESS

A lady of whom I remember little beyond the fact that she gave me a beautiful doll's tea-set was Miss Camilla Croudace. She lived on Marley and was the retired Head Mistress of Queen's College, Harley Street, to which Mother went as a schoolgirl. She had been a great and cultured "Lady Resident" who attracted specialists in their subjects as lecturers to her college. There is no doubt that the standard was very high and the girls responded to their treatment as students rather than schoolgirls. Gertrude Bell, the well-known traveller and worker for Middle East stability had been there just before Mother.

I enjoyed as a girl of about nine or ten, the few visits I paid to her home because of her understanding and lack of patronage. I felt at ease and very grateful for the magnificent present. I played with it only on "best occasions," and kept it a long time.

TOYS A RARITY

Toys in our family were somewhat classified according to their worth. Of everyday toys there were few by modern standards. Building bricks of all shapes and sizes formed the basis of much indoor play, and of course I had my china doll kept well away from teasing brothers. For the most part we had the great outdoors and the barns. But come a cold, wet day or Sunday evening and we might get out our specials and play with them on the table.

Mother had many pieces of a doll's dinner service in delicate willow pattern china, and some dear little glass tumblers. These were got out very occasionally to be admired and then wrapped in tissue paper and put away again. I still have these pieces.

Who owned the Noah's Ark, I do not remember. Possibly Father had bought it as a Sunday toy for us all. It came out after tea and we arranged the animals in the conventional two by two. They were quite large and well made in wood covered in what must have been real hide. How choice are wooden toys compared to the plastic of modern times.

An every-day outdoor toy belonging to Hugh and Mary was a low trolley big enough for one child to sit in and be pulled along by the other. This Father bought at Gamages on a pre-Christmas shopping excursion in which I was included. How exciting it was to see the huge store and to see Father actually spending a lot of money, for we lived under the impression that we were always poor and must not ask for anything. The trolley packed with other presents stood in the corridor as we returned home by train in the dark winter evening.

Again my chapter has wandered. We have visited our shop, our governess, our various neighbours, but how good it is to return to the cosiness of our own hearth, particularly at Christmas time.

Jonathan Hutchinson in his museum at Haslemere

DOWN TO HASLEMERE

"Smack went the whip,
 Round went the wheels
 Were never folk so glad,
 The stones they rattled underneath …"

William Cowper

We drove carefully down Shepherd's Hill into Haslemere

DOWN TO HASLEMERE

EARLY COMMUNICATIONS

The telephone and car have made life spin along so much faster now-a-days that it is extraordinary to think how much we accomplished without either. But life is all a matter of relative values and although probably more forethought was given to our links with the civilised world away from our hill-top, it was not all that slow and uncertain.

We knew we should have a reply to a postcard by the next morning. If an engagement or some piece of news was more urgent there was always the telegraph boy. It was not easy for us to send telegrams for they had to be handed in at Haslemere Post Office. But on occasion we received them, generally with a feeling of apprehension until they were opened.

Telegraph boys wore dark blue suits with a pill-box hat kept on jauntily with a strap under the chin. A leather belt held in place a little case in which the orange coloured envelope was kept safely. Off they pedalled on their red bicycles all over the town and the surrounding country.

While the telegram was being opened the delivery boy waited politely at the door. One could send an answer back by the boy who took it to the Post Office, or one merely said "No answer" and sent him on his way, if he was lucky with a tip of two or three coppers.

Apart from shopping excursions, visits to relations and for the adults not infrequent days in London, we had few engagements to keep. In cases of illness the doctor called at the house. There were surgeries, but these were not intended for the likes of us. We paid for what we had for this was long before the National Health Service. I do not think my parents ever sat in a doctor's waiting-room.

After the initial smallpox vaccination children had no other jabs. Medical science has done wonderful work in stamping out polio, diphtheria and T.B. since those days and in lessening the effects of other infectious illnesses such as measles and mumps.

The dentist, of course, had to be visited, but I only went twice in the whole of my childhood, once when I was about eight (and the filling soon came out again) and again, when in my teens I had raging tooth-ache and had a tooth removed late at night.

Father knew exactly how long it took him to walk from **A** to **B**. Taking for the moment **A** to be Moses Hill and **B** the station he would set off at exactly the time it needed, probably forty minutes, and reached there with just time to buy his ticket and walk quickly over the bridge to the up line. The train was signalled if not already pulling up. Father hated *waste of time,* and one way of wasting time was standing on a draughty platform. This was alright if he alone was concerned, but some of us arrived rather breathless and anxious.

The journey to London took about an hour and a half, as compared with fifty minutes now, but you got your money's worth, for on Wednesdays there was a cheap ticket of half-a-crown return. Father went to London on business concerned with his building and brick and tile works, and on one occasion he took me to the docks somewhere down in the East End where he was choosing imported timber. He also went quite often to the London Library of which he was a life member.

THE ROAD TO HASLEMERE

Most of our little excursions, however, were with Mother to Hasle-mere. For these the pony had to be caught and harnessed and certain children rounded up and made tidy. George Parvin dealt with the pony-trap while Phoebe or Matoo scrubbed our faces and saw that we had clean hankies. If in haste, we were let off with a "lick-and-a-promise." Phoebe would put a little spit – either hers or mine – on a handkerchief and rub the dirty marks away. Mother changed into a coat and skirt or a dress, and always a hat. Headgear was worn by all, kiddies and grown-ups too, all the year round. There was no slipping into town in one's old clothes to buy something in a hurry. It was a well-planned expedition and took the whole afternoon.

If Mother was driving she would pass the reins to me for a while along the quiet road from Kingsley Green to the bridge over the stream at "The Sussex Bell" where we crossed into Surrey. The road was still quiet but getting more hilly for the next mile, and Mother would soon take control again to get us safely up and down the hills.

On one occasion straw had been laid on the road outside "Dene End Farm," a handsome Georgian house standing back in its garden behind a wall. I was told someone was very ill there and traffic must pass as quietly as possible. The clippety-clop of the horse's hooves on the hard stony road was the worst that could be expected, and there was not all that traffic on the road in any case.

Roads were metalled with small stones rolled in by a steam-roller with lots of water. Immediately after resurfacing they were covered in fine slimy mud. This mostly settled in with use, but roads were always muddy in wet weather, while in dry weather dust blew off them, covering the hedges with a white film. Our pony, *Kit,* hated the steam-roller and tended to shy. He had to be urged gently past.

A common sight was of a man sitting on the grass verge breaking up stones that had been dropped there in a great heap ready for filling in holes or resurfacing the road. Crack, crack, crack went the hammer of the road-mender all day long, till the pile was all reduced to the same size, roughly three inches across. Our local sandstone was soft, so for main roads a hard grey limestone was brought in.

LOCAL SHOPKEEPERS

After something around half-an-hour we reached our metropolis, Haslemere. There was, of course, shopping to do. This did not interest me much but I remember as we approached the town down picturesque Shepherd's Hill seeing stout, rosy-faced Mr Rogers standing in the doorway of his corn-merchant's facing us. And as we left the town by the same route seeing the other side of the picture: dour little Mr Purkiss guarding the entrance to *his* corn-merchant's right in the angle of Shepherds Hill and Lower Street. He wore breeches and shiny leather gaiters. His high, rather ugly building has long since gone. The two rivals stood almost opposite each other. We patronised both. The smell of cow-cake and grain was pleasantly like our own barns at home, and we usually went back with a sack of corn for the hens if nothing more.

Along High Pavement (alias Lower Street, of course) we would visit two shops. One was the grocer's, Waterstons, which had a wider selection of goods than our little village shop at Kingsley Green. Of course, all business was transacted over the counter. One never thought of helping oneself off the shelves, and in any case everything except what was on display in the window was kept well behind the counter. There would be one or two chairs on which a weary customer could sit and have a little chat while discussing the merits of this and that commodity.

Thompsons, the Northampton Shoe Shop, was a dark little cobbler's, smelling of leather and heelball. Here we were measured for new boots, for they were often made specially for us. As a tit-bit of geography Father told us that Northampton was the home of the shoe and boot manufacturing industry in England, and this piece of knowledge actually stuck.

Haslemere High Street was quite a busy place

Materials for dresses were bought by the yard and made up at home. Underclothes were generally bought ready-made. There were several shops to choose from but they did not interest me sufficiently to remain in my memory. Mother, so far as I recollect, chose the materials; I accepted with resignation. Few clothes interested me though a red velvet dress really pleased me very much. I did not mind that it was a hand-down from a cousin. Looking at photographs of this period it is evident that some of my artistic aunts made frocks for me. They have artistically embroidered yokes, very "Aunt Ursularish."

It was too far for me to venture to Haslemere alone, and for a very long time I was shy of going into shops. The older boys, of course, had bicycles and were much more independent, and until they went to boarding school, went daily to Mr Oldaker's prep. school.

Jan was a real "farmer's boy" and nothing pleased him more than to help on the farm. He felt no end grown-up when he accompanied Parvin or Mr Wheeler on foot to collect some cows that had come by train to Haslemere Station. Walking them back, they stopped for a rest and sat on a bank to eat their "bait", chunks of bread and cheese. This Jan cut and lifted to his mouth with his sturdy penknife in imitation of his companion. How good it must have tasted, the staple mid-day snack of the farm labourer.

Jan grew up with a love of the land and emigrated to New Zealand. By a series of unfortunate circumstances, chief of which was the severe earthquake of 1931 which cracked his farm almost to pieces and rendered his house uninhabitable just at the time of world-wide depression, he, with his young wife, Nell, and their new-born baby were forced home again and farming very reluctantly abandoned.

The Sweet shop, always a great attraction.
The dress and toys are typical of the time.

THE HASLEMERE MUSEUM

Occasionally Father would take us down to the town on a Sunday afternoon to visit the Museum. This had been founded by Grandfather in 1888 and was largely arranged by him with the help of E W Swanton, the curator. It was unique in being an Educational Museum. It was then on Museum Hill and Grandfather might be giving a lecture. These talks attracted many interested adults including the rector, G H Aitken, for they ranged over such a wide variety of topics that there was something for everybody. There would be references to poets and poetry, to history, geology, zoology and evolution. He showed specimens and literally "found sermons in stones." Often the talks were given out of doors, the audience sitting on a grassy slope. They loved it.

'One might stroke the kangaroo ...'

We children were rather young for this strong meat and roamed the museum galleries alone. There was a ghoulish fascination in gazing at the kitten with two heads, and the Siamese twin chicks (bottled) and one or two other monstrosities. This kind of interest, however, was frowned upon by our parents, producing a "guilt complex," though we didn't know it. Rather frightening was the crocodile that lurked on the floor under one of the cabinets. Its open, toothy jaws were much too close to one's feet. We were also rather scared of Mr Swanton, the curator. He was devoted to Grandfather but had little use for his grandchildren. He would appear from nowhere, and one had the feeling that he was gently "moving one on." I was happy in the bird gallery. There was a case of humming birds that could be admired again and again, and a fine upstanding bustard in a large case. It was our boast that Uncle Roger, who liked a bit of pheasant shooting, had shot the last one in the country and this was it. What a wicked boast! And how entirely without foundation for bustards had been extinct since 1830.

There were swing frames in the History gallery containing articles and illustrations of historical and archaeological discoveries. They were on stands and one turned one frame round to the next like the pages of a book. There was far too much to absorb and we contented ourselves with idly rotating the frames. The busts of people like Aristotle and Homer I disliked because, like all statues everywhere, they looked blind.

One might stroke the kangaroo, standing up boldly taller than oneself – if one dared. As the kangaroo became stroked of most of its fur it was replaced by a large brown bear. These were appealing to small children, for they tested their courage.

More seriously they bore out the principle that marked the museum as different from all others in that it was definitely educational. Education involved the use of all senses, and there were a number of objects that could be handled. It was unfortunate that I was just too young to take part in the Museum Examinations held periodically for local children, for they really did open the eyes and minds of many to the possibilities of educating oneself in a museum.

Perhaps the object that we, along with countless children since, ogled at most was the Egyptian mummy. Ghoulish, yes, but this time an allowable morbidity, for it was historical, and Father was almost fanatical about history. So we looked at the dirty rags, outlining the shape of head, body and legs, and then at the toes, yes *real* toes sticking out at the end. "Horrid" many would say, but we held it in horrid fascination.

The afternoon wore on slowly as Grandfather held his audience in rapt attention, and my legs began to ache and my head to long for the freshness of our hill-top. Alas, one day before we were re-claimed by our parents disaster fell. Tired and bored I leant too heavily on a glass case and broke it. Mr Swanton as usual appeared from nowhere and I was in sore disgrace. My chief worry was that Father would have to pay, I did not know *how* much, to have it mended. In fact I dare say he didn't pay anything, but, oh dear, how disgraced I felt.

It is sad to give this picture of the Museum that in its unique way has become almost world famous, and of which I am now proud to be the Hutchinson Trustee. It has evolved into something much more attractive and instructive to children for the exhibits are not over-loaded, and there are many things for a child to do, and the curator and his staff are welcoming and ready to help at any level.

Mr Swanton enjoyed this same reputation with most people, but I think he had a fear of being criticised by his employer's sons, my father and uncles, and tended to keep them at bay. There were probably faults on both sides. He certainly was a very great naturalist and his books *A Country Museum, A Country Calendar* as well as his book *British Galls* are still well worth reading.

Inval valley in 1889.
'Aunt Elsie' called this photograph 'The Happy Valley'.

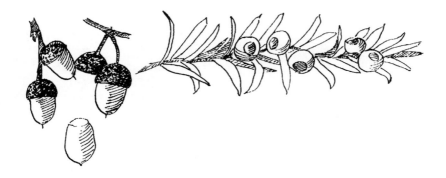

OVER TO INVAL

She loved her garden as an artist viewing it, as a naturalist making it, most of all … for the Creator at work in the world, the miracle of resurrection every spring-time.

Sir George Newman
about Auntie Elsie Newman

Grandfather (L) at the Moat, Inval

OVER TO INVAL

GRANDFATHER AND RELATIVES

A mile beyond Haslemere brought us to Inval, the beautiful hilly estate owned by Grandfather Jonathan Hutchinson. Here were two houses full it seemed of elderly relations. Of course the aunts were not really old, but to a small child anyone who had put their hair up and wore long skirts was surrounded by the aura of adulthood and was treated with the respect always accorded to the older generation.

By the time I remember, Inval House the first Haslemere home of the Hutchinsons, had been given up some years. It was leased to Mr Bromley who had a boys' cramming school. The ousted Hutchinsons were moving uphill, nearer Heaven.

Halfway up the hill was "High Inval" in which lived Mother's mother, Grandmother Woods, and her two unmarried daughters, Aunt Kitty of photographic and cricketing fame, and Aunt Hilda who played and sang Gilbert and Sullivan songs with us. We loved these aunts and there will be more about them anon. Sharing the same house was frail Aunt Alice Hutchinson accompanied by her spinster daughter Cousin Truda. She was "Cousin" to us as she was of our parents' generation. A sweet person, full of quaint little jokes, she was also always ready to show me a bird's nest or little wild flowers. She was a good naturalist. There had been other daughters but two had died a few years ago, and others, and little boys also, in childhood. There was only Oswald (sorry Cousin Oswald) left and he was doing something on the Great Northern Railway, tapping the wheels as the train stood in the station he told us, but we didn't believe him. Both Grandmother and Aunt Alice were widows. One would think that this was enough for one house considering that each side had a resident maid. These servants lived together and probably shared an attic bedroom, and although they cooked separate meals they shared the same coal range. But Grandmother also had living with her her only unmarried sister,

Deborah. She was Aunt Debbie to us and I am sorry to say I only remember her portrait, for she had ringlets. She died in 1909 having spent much time in recent years alone in her bedroom (all meals carried up of course), with some mysterious complaint, depression we should now call it.

In 1911, after paying one or two visits from New Zealand, Uncle Arthur finally filled the gap in the household.

'The Library' at Inval. This picture by 'Aunt Elsie'
was probably taken in the 1890s.

Further up the hill at the house called "The Library" lived Grandfather himself, also with two daughters, Aunts Ursula and Agnes. Grandfather was tall and stately despite a slight stoop. He had a shaggy beard and wore steel-rimmed spectacles halfway down his nose. We were somewhat in awe of him due to his greatness as a medical man, a fact Father never let us forget. He still dropped certain h's, not through lack of education, but retaining an old-fashioned, rather aristocratic custom. He referred to 'otels, and 'umour, and annoyed poor Hugh by calling him "Ue." I am sure, however, he never said 'Utchinson.

In 1908 he was knighted, though years earlier he had refused a peerage. To commemorate this event we were each given a photograph. There was a choice between a portrait and one where he was seated wearing court dress and holding a curious hat. This was the costume he had worn as he knelt before the King and was touched on the shoulder and bidden to "rise, Sir Jonathan Hutchinson." It was breath-taking to think of! Looking at the two photographs I longed for this one for the honour and glory of it all, but felt it would be conceited to ask for it, so chose the other. It was certainly the better likeness.

There was no need to be afraid of Grandfather for he was very kind and gentle. Each Christmas he gave a grandchildren's party at which we were given quite extravagant presents. These were hidden around the rooms and we had to hunt for the one with our name on it. One year I had a little white muff and tippet. Alas, alas, I lost the muff on the way home in the dark. How awful!

No doubt Aunt Ursula, who kept house for Grandfather, did all the organising of these parties and got none of the thank-yous from us children. I think our parents were well aware of her selfless devotion. She did not generally give us Christmas or birthday presents herself, but if she knew there was something we really wanted that would help us in our hobbies, she gave it. Thus it was, a little later, that I got my first good bird book and binoculars. It was most thoughtful of her, for bird-watching was not her interest at all. She was a beautiful embroideress and later on a weaver of some fame.

Aunt Agnes we really were afraid of! She was very tall, and although there was a gleam in her eye, her tongue could make the clever, caustic comment. She was an H. M. I. (Her Majesty's Inspector), a daunting title indeed. I fancy she could put the fear of God into any hesitant young teacher, though she would come home with many amusing stories. These of course never reached the ears of us youngsters. They were strictly for adults only. The generation gap was wide indeed, and the phrase "one's elders and betters" freely used.

THE PARTIES

The Grandchildren's party was no exception to the rule that the children had to perform for the benefit (?) of these elders and betters, and this was rather a damper. For weeks beforehand Mother was teaching my reluctant self a poem to recite. One year it was "When Polly Buys a Hat." It was a stupid thing of three or four verses and Mother insisted on my saying it with *feeling,* and with actions. My hands must go up to show the size of the brim; they must go down again and out at some exclamation. I forget the details.

But I knew when it came to the moment of truth that Mother would be helpless and I would have my way.

My name was called. I emerged from the crowd of cousins and

walked a few steps up the stairs and turned to face them all. Then with hands held firmly down each side recited the whole thing in a perfectly wooden voice. Mother was furious, but it was too late. I had won.

A not too clever game we all enjoyed was Family Coach. Each one chose part of the coach set-up as his own: the front wheels, the whip, the lamps, the driver, father's top hat, etc. Then one of the aunts would tell a hair-raising story of the family coach returning from a party. There would be deep mud, the front wheels came off (up jumped the front wheels and turned round), there was a pond the horse fell in, (up got the horse after a bit of prompting, and did his turn around), father's hat floated away ("hat, hat" would be shouted at some small child who had forgotten his part) and so the story proceeded from one disaster to another, including of course the highwaymen on Gibbet Hill.

Driving home on the dark winter's night after this lively end to the party was quite part of the excitement. We wrapped rugs round our legs, but the three mile journey in our open dog-cart seemed very long, and more than one of us had a few shudders as we drove carefully past Inval Pond where the road was narrow and there was no hedge or fence between it and the water. Our two oil lamps cast an eerie light along the tree-lined roads and we thought again of those highwaymen on Hindhead who had killed a sailor and been hanged on Gibbet Hill, a spot we knew well on bright, sunny days. But we always arrived home safely – except for that muff!

Sometimes other aunts gave parties. Aunt Elsie Newman gave a grand evening party soon after Christmas in her lovely old house, "Hazelhurst," in Bunch Lane. We also visited her quite often during the summer when her spacious garden was a joy to explore.

"HAZELHURST" AND BUNCH LANE

Aunt Elsie and Uncle Tom were gardeners of the Gertrude Jekyll age. Tastefully laid out, the garden looked natural. The lawn was like velvet and at one end rose a magnificent Cedar of Lebanon. In this tree, slung neatly under a branch one spring, we found the tiny nest of the Goldcrest. There was a bird-bath on a pedestal which formed the centre-piece of many photographs of happy children taken by Aunt Elsie or Aunt Kitty. These enterprising people were doing their own developing, printing and enlarging.

Away at the other end of the lawn was a small goldfish pond, while along one side glowed a herbaceous border and on the other a glade of rhododendrons and azaleas amongst which one wandered at will.

Years later I met a couple of Friends (Quakers) who told me how, when they were first married, they had stayed at "Hazelhurst." On looking out of their bedroom window in the early morning they were enchanted to see a pheasant walking on the lawn. If only they could see one on the lawn of the new house they were about to settle in in Suffolk, the picture would be complete they said to each other.

On waking up the first morning in their new home ... but need I finish? Their cup was filled. These worthy Friends were the Allens of the Allen and Hanbury Chemists' firm, and they too cultivated a beautiful garden inspired, I like to think, by the visit to "Hazelhurst."

'Hazelhurst' garden, probably in the 1890s

The rose garden at "Hazelhurst" was formal and hallowed for Uncle Tom experimented in grafting roses. He did not achieve fame for this as did his brother-in-law Allen Chandler, living at the other end of Bunch Lane, also with a beautiful garden. The glowing red 'Allen Chandler' climber has been listed in rose catalogues for many years. One of the finest specimens I ever saw was in the 1960s at Sissinghurst in Kent. My own plant is still flourishing in 1980.

Aunt Elsie was the typical Edwardian, one might almost say Victorian, lady gardener. In her long, full dress covered with a spacious cotton print apron and large straw hat she would sally forth through the french windows with a flat flower basket to "dead-head" the borders and cut flowers for the house. Flower arranging as such had yet to be invented but the bunches of mixed colours in large Italian pots and bowls lent grace to the beautifully yet simply, furnished rooms. She was tall and walked with a peculiarly springing step. One felt happy beside her.

Uncle Tom was small and had little to say to children. He travelled daily to London where he had a firm of printers. Sometimes he walked to the station a mile away, sometimes he rode horse-back. Then his gardener would walk up to bring the horse home. Alas, one day in 1914 as he was waiting on the platform he collapsed and died.

Aunt Elsie continued to live at "Hazelhurst" and on several occasions very kindly "stood" our poor family a sea-side holiday. She had no children of her own but adopted, though not legally, an orphaned brother and sister, Arthur and Margot Craddock. Margot stayed with her and cared for her in her last illness in 1927.

Uncle Allen Chandler was our Aunt Ethel Hutchinson's husband. Mother and Aunt Ethel liked to share confidences, but I felt shy of her. She always seemed rather sad, and a little lacking in a sense of humour. I am sure she had no idea how funny she was being when, at the tea-table, she would say: "There's bread on the side if anyone wants jam."

This became a byword that leant itself to endless variations by frivolous nephews and nieces. It was not allowed, even in her elegant home, to eat butter and jam together, and there was always a plate of thin bread and butter on the table.

Though one did not speak to Uncle Allen unless spoken to, he was rather fun to be near. He was very different from our other relations. Most of them had Quaker blood running through their veins, even if some were watering it down with Church of England. Uncle Allen was County (Surrey!). Having "arrived" (County Cricket and a J.P.) he could afford to wear the shabbiest of tweed clothes and talk with an exaggerated drawl through his soup-strainer moustache.

"Paass the maamaalaade" he would say, and we loved to hear it. Sitting on the floor by him at table was a slobbering old spaniel. "Doown, Sammy, down," he drawled, hitting the dog on the head with the spoon as he served out the rice pudding. Aunt Ethel looked pained, but it really was rather refreshing.

Legend has it that when he was living at Stroud House near Grayswood, he once pulled the communication cord in the down train from London, hopped off and walked across the field home to save the bother of going on to Haslemere station.

Another juicy tale is of Uncle Allen looking like a tramp complete with a bag over his shoulder, trudging over the fields and opening a gate to let a gentleman on horse-back through. He was offered, and accepted, a sixpenny tip. That evening, suitably dressed, they found themselves sitting opposite each other at a grand dinner-party.

He had a habit of filling his pockets with apples to give to children. He would wait in Farnham Lane to give some to little Mrs Backwell as she walked home. He called her The Merry Widow, for she was still young and pretty. Years later she too joined our family circle by marrying Uncle Roger. She was in her seventies and he was eighty-five and sadly only lived four months after their marriage.

There were three Chandler offspring, Allen (Rex), Katherine and Prunella (Prue). They were older than our lot. Like their mother they were intensely artistic and Rex and Katherine took over the pantomime started by Aunt Ursula and developed it into a unique play which ran until the Second World War killed it dead.

Father's Quakerly outlook forbade our taking part, though Mother managed to smuggle George in once when he was a young boy. He was a "forty thief." Father considered that some of his brothers and sisters spent too much time on amateur dramatics, but they certainly did them with great artistry and good taste. On one occasion, when Aunt Hilda was twenty-seven and was playing Dick Whittington there were great heart-searchings with her mother as to whether her skirt should be just above or just below the knee.

DANCING LESSONS

Although acting was denied me I did attend Katherine's weekly dancing class. Gwen Raverat, in her book about the Darwins, *Period Piece,* relates her hatred of dancing classes and all that went with them. Beyond feeling overgrown and clumsy I did not mind them so much and really enjoyed the dumb-bells we swung around in various exercises to music. We learnt the polka, the gallop and the waltz, and I mastered them at basic level. Praise was seldom given so I felt a real uplift when I overheard Katherine telling Mother that I was very good at dumb-bells. This was probably said in mitigation of the rest of the lesson, but I was grateful for any small crumbs. Probably praise was only given for real achievement. A hard trier was not recognised. And how careful both Katherine and Mother were not to tell *me*. I wonder why?

The dancing lessons qualified one to go to parties more advanced than mere children's parties. While we were at Moses Hill, I was rather young for these, but later on I endured a "dance" given by Miss Nettie Whymper for her niece Ethel, the daughter of the climber of Matterhorn fame, Edward. Shy and plain I sat most of the evening as a "wallflower" and decided once and for all that dances were not for me.

Summer parties took place generally in one or other of the lovely gardens. One organised by Katherine ended in disgrace, for after tea we were divided into two teams and told to prepare and act a short scene, I think from History. A few clothes were put out and we might collect sticks and brushwood from the copse at the bottom of the garden. This was asking for trouble. We had little imagination or inclination, and several of the little boys, some of my brothers included, turned it into a rag, making good use of the sticks. They giggled and larked about and refused to take it seriously. Katherine was very cross and we were glad to depart home, I am afraid quite unrepentant.

A party more to our liking was the annual Hay Party at "Silverdale," the home of the Coventry girls. The eldest, Joan, married Rex and so came into our family. This party was informal, we made houses and castles in the hay and had a delicious tea.

Best of all were the real hay-making parties at Mills' farm at Kingsley Green. Here whole families of Mills and their friends turned out working and playing together. Many of the women and girls wore the old-fashioned sun-bonnets, and I had one too.

Those who could, tossed the hay to dry it, raked it into long rows across the field, made the rows into hay-cocks, and finally loaded it onto the hay-wains that plodded, horse-drawn of course, back and forth to the stack-yard. Mothers brought baskets of scrunchy home-made scones and cakes and these were washed down with cold tea.

SUNDAY ACTIVITIES

Reference has been made to Sunday games at home. These came late in the day. Every Sunday morning, unless the weather was impossible, dressed in our best we set off for Friends Meeting at Inval. There was no "Need I go?" It was taken for granted that *this was done*. The boys wore dark suits with stiff, white collars, and I wore, while it fitted me, my red velvet frock with a lacy petticoat under it. My hair, generally shoulder-length, was well brushed and kept off my face with a velvet band.

The trek from Moses Hill to Inval was a good three miles and we resorted to various ways of compassing it. The pony-trap was reserved for Mother and those too young to cycle, while Father and the older boys bicycled. Babies were left at home in Phoebe's care. We started going to Meeting at about four or five years old.

There was no Sunday School and we sat as patiently as possible for the whole hour. Somehow the relaxed silence of the gathering, and hopefully some of its hidden meaning, entered our young selves so that the time, though long, was not so difficult to bear as one might think. Some young children brought "Sunday books" to look at, and I remember watching our little cousin Kathleen Rosher eating "pretend" strawberries from a picture in her book. The Meeting House was a curious little wooden building, bark-covered timbers outside lined with pitch-board boarding. It had housed the first Haslemere Museum founded by Grandfather in 1888. When this was moved to larger premises in Haslemere the Friends took it over. Most of those attending Meeting for Worship were of the Hutchinson tribe, but a few others were attracted.

Uncle Tom Newman, as an Elder, sat facing the Meeting with one or two others. There was some ministry, most of which passed over my head. How embarrassed we felt when Uncle Tom, evidently trying to catch the attention of the children, stood up and began relating the well-known Old Testament story by saying "When Samuel was a boy, about the age of Jan there ..." On one occasion there was something caught in a groove in the wall. It moved convulsively now and then as if trying to free itself. It was a bat. We continued our silent worship notwithstanding until Uncle Tom and his neighbour had drawn the Meeting to a close by shaking hands, and then we gathered round the poor little animal. Father gently released it and we had a good look at it before letting it out of the building.

Many, many years later a younger generation of children were kept quietly entertained at Godalming Meeting watching several tiny frogs hopping about the floor. They had come in under the door. Again no action was taken until Meeting ended.

After Meeting we took turns at going to dinner with Grandmother Woods and Aunts Kitty and Hilda. "High Inval" was just up the hill and we walked up a little path across the field and into their garden. Two of us went at a time so that we had company in walking home again. We always enjoyed these visits for the aunts were very understanding of children and were full of fun. On wet days there were indoor games and puzzles and singing round the piano. In the summer we played in the garden which was a simple affair, mostly grass, unlike the more pretentious ones of the Newmans and Chandlers. There was Bumble Puppy and croquet and a seat in a large clump of Portugal Laurel that made a splendid "house", and odd corners for hide-and-seek. There were dogs and cats and, if we were very subdued a visit to Uncle Arthur's studio to watch him working with hammer and chisel.

We might go for a walk down to The Moat, a clear, cold pool in the wood across a couple of fields. In winter we wound our way down a drift of snowdrops, growing so profusely they almost obliterated the little path. Aunt Ursula had planted the original bulbs but they had spread and become a carpet of white for some twenty yards or more. By spring a gorgeous red rhododendron that was growing high into an oak tree was dropping dead flowers into the water. Also growing close to the water was the rare Royal Fern *(Osmunda regale)*. It is interesting to add as a footnote here, that in years to come The Moat became very overshadowed by trees and the Royal Fern disappeared. When in the 1970s considerable clearing was done it reappeared in just the same spot. Apparently it is a fern that likes to grow on the spring line and that is exactly its situation there. There are strong springs within The Moat which keep the water very cold. It was said that the only person who would bathe in it was Grandfather, who sometimes took a morning dip and out again quickly.

The Moat in winter, 1889

We walked all round this long narrow pool looking for trout and occasionally finding a moorhen's nest. The ram went thud, thud, thud all the time. This was pumping water to all the houses on the Inval Estate, and beautiful water it was. Years later it fell into disuse and "mains" water arrived, and of course, had to be paid for.

These visits to "High Inval" were certainly happy and relaxed. Grandmother was a sweet old lady, and Aunt Alice living on the other side of the house, was another. They wore dark dresses, grey or black with a little white lace round the neck, and a lace cap. Very often a crocheted shawl to keep off draughts was added. Outdoors in summer they wore large dark, shady hats. They took little walks about the garden and through the field marked on the map as the Soldiers' Field, but known to us as the rabbit field as there was an enormous rabbit warren. We would go to the gate and clap our hands to see the hundreds of rabbits, white scuts a-bobbing, bolt for their holes.

Grandfather had planted a line of trees, laburnum and Norway maple, across the field to give shade to what was called, if you retained your Yorkshire accent "The Ants' Path," or to us southerners "The Arnts' Parth." These little walks were accompanied by their daughters on whose arms the old ladies might lean. Aunt Alice took to a bath (or barth) chair for she was supposed to be tubercular and had lost most of her large family that way. But she outlived Grandmother by fifteen years.

UNCLE ARTHUR

Compared to the "senior citizens" of today careering around in our cars, hatless and in slacks, they seem extremely aged. Yet Grandmother was only sixty-nine when she died at Bormes in South France in 1913, whither she had gone in an attempt to throw off bronchial pneumonia. Aunt Alice had a trained nurse, Nurse Lowe, in attendance for the last ten years of her life. She was in poor circumstances financially as her husband, Edward Hutchinson, had failed both in business and in health and had fled to South America in an unsuccessful search for the latter. He had died there in 1884. Kind Uncle Arthur, Edward's youngest brother, quietly paid for the nurse.

He had returned from New Zealand, where unbeknown to anyone, he had amassed a fair fortune. A bachelor, he came to stay with Grandmother and Aunts Kitty and Hilda in 1911 ... and just stayed. He never asked their leave but, such were the strong family ties, and so silent was he about his affairs, that no one dared to ask how he intended to spend his retirement.

He was no trouble. He contributed towards the house-keeping and required a boiled egg for breakfast every morning. He also had a little (very little) wine with his meal, which Aunt Kitty bought him and "winked at," for the household otherwise was teetotal. One day, after being there several years, he put a cheque in her hand saying gruffly, "A little towards my wine." No wine account had been kept, but a hundred pounds in those days was something indeed.

Inevitably I am running on beyond the Moses Hill days, but some of these elderly relatives' stories must be wound up.

Uncle Arthur would say through his beard one day: "I think I will go and see Kathleen for a few days," and he would take himself off with practically no luggage to his niece Kathleen Hurst, at Bexhill-on-Sea. Then one of the aunts would write a hasty note to Kathleen asking her to let them know if he showed any signs of returning. Apparently this was assumed when Kathleen saw him writing a postcard.

It was said that once he had been sweet on Kathleen, the daughter of Mark Hutchinson. Could an uncle ask his niece's hand in marriage? Perhaps he felt not. Anyway, lively pretty Kathleen married Saxby Hurst, and Uncle Arthur went to New Zealand.

My childish recollection of Cousin Kathleen was of her deafness. She would thrust an instrument like a large box camera at one and ask some quite ordinary question that rendered one speechless. If it wasn't the box camera it was a long speaking tube that was just as alarming. Like the other widows she too had a "daughter-in-waiting," Muriel, with very much her mother's lively manner and lovely blue, blue eyes. Alec, her son went back to Africa where his grandfather had made his home, though he appeared now and then as well as keeping in touch by mail.

To return to Uncle Arthur. In his retirement at "High Inval" he spent much of his time doing exquisite wood-work, some of which is still about. I use daily a dear little plant stand made by him. During the First World War he made bed-tables and other useful accessories for the Haslemere Hospital.

He was nursed dutifully by Aunts Kitty and Hilda as he grew old and frail, and he died at "High Inval" in 1928. It was not until his will was read with some ceremony by his solicitor that the assembled relations, including my parents, realised something of his wealth. Thousands of pounds lay idle in his current account; the rest was in property in New Zealand. His assets were divided into twelve equal shares, one for each family of his brothers and sisters, except for Jonathan, who had plenty anyway. There was one exception. A whole share was left to *each* of the Woods sisters. It was hard to take all this in as it was read out, until Uncle Roger whispered to Mother: "That means you."

It took forty years to wind up the estate and new trustees had to be appointed as old ones died off. The numerous nephews and nieces and their offspring were scattered all over the world, and sometimes it was difficult to trace them. Jan was one of the last trustees.

For our family, it was the turning point as regards our financial balance. Mother and Father were so used to living economically that it was ingrained in them and they never cast it off. It was not until Mother's death in 1960 that I realised at last that I had no need to be *too* careful. What a relief!

'The Croft House' in 1997.

Aunt Kitty and Aunt Hilda, together with Cousin Truda and her brother Oswald who was due to retire from the railway up north, built "The Croft House" in the field above "High Inval" with their new-found wealth in 1930, and all lived there for the remainder of their lives. Aunt Hilda was the last to go, and I lived with her for the last eight years of her life and bought the west end of the house from the estate after her death in 1971.

OTHER RELATIVES

We have not finished with Moses Hill yet, however, so back we go, toiling up that last steep bit after one of our frequent visits to Inval.

And now that we have been introduced to our many aunts we can picture constant visits, particularly by Aunt Kitty and Aunt Hilda. Some time around 1912 a bus started to run from Haslemere out to Kingsley Green. At first it was just a taxi, but was soon "the brown bus." Though this was a great innovation, it was not to be relied upon too often, for on occasion it could be hired for the day, and off it would go to the sea-side or the races.

Occasionally on Sunday one of the aunts would bring along Cousin Joe. We had probably seen him at Meeting in the morning and were all excited as preparations for a big family tea were in progress.

J A Woods (what initials for a dentist!) was "pure Woods," a cousin of Mother's with no Hutchinson blood, as most of them had. "Pure Woods's" were known for their wonderful sense of humour. Father once said that Mother's father, George Woods, was the funniest man he had ever known. Cousin Joe must have been like him.

He was a very successful dentist in Liverpool and when he came to London for conferences spent the week-end at "High Inval."

Rotund, with a big smiling face and immaculately dressed for the city, he nevertheless enjoyed country walking and the opportunity to trudge up to our hill-top, where he was assured of a good audience for his funny stories. He greeted each of his female cousins with a whacking great kiss and a hug. There was nothing half-hearted or reserved about Cousin Joe. Was this the splash of Irish blood in him? He was quite a contrast to the reserved English Hutchinsons.

Formalities (some formal!) over, we sat down to tea prepared to enjoy ourselves to the full. But first he would settle himself a few inches away from the table and explain: "When I touch I know I've had enough." We bowed our heads in silent grace. After a moment there was a little falsetto "Amen" and he would look round the table to see which of us had said it. Mother and Father exchanged looks and tried not to laugh; we were all grinning broadly. From then on it was one joke or funny story after another, and how we laughed! Only did the danger flag go up if Father and Cousin Joe got on to politics, for both could get decidedly hot under the collar. Then Aunt Kitty would say loudly to Mother, "How's Baby, Ella" to change the subject and cool the air.

Grandmother thought some of his jokes just a wee bit vulgar. He *would* refer to the pork pie she always got for Sunday supper as "swine tart." History does not relate what silent Uncle Arthur made of these lively interludes, but the aunts enjoyed them hugely. I am not sure, either, just how amused Cousin Joe himself was one dark, wet night when he was returning alone from Moses Hill and fell in a ditch in Bunch Lane. A policeman found him groping for his bowler hat and a galosh and helped to retrieve them, but wondered...? Cousin Joe was a strict teetotaller and a man of exemplary conduct.

His gracious wife, Cousin Madge, seldom came down to Haslemere but Mother once took me to visit them in their beautiful home in Liverpool. They kept two Irish maids and on Saturday afternoons had a few friends in for tennis. Tea, with dainty cucumber sandwiches, cakes and strawberries and cream on the lawn was elegant but none the less acceptable. One was introduced to the refinements of Edwardian life without feeling awkward or shy for the garden echoed with laughter. We visited Cousin Joe's father and mother, stout, elderly bodies rippling with mirth. Uncle William, as he was to me, was inevitably associated in my mind with Lewis Carroll's "You are old Father William." He fitted the bill exactly.

I rather blotted my copy-book on that visit to Liverpool, for knowing Cousin Joe's fondness for jokes, I hid his slippers while he was out. He did not come home till after I was in bed and asleep, and was not amused. What I did not realise was that it was *his* jokes he enjoyed, not mine.

Grandmother Woods with the Rosher triplets: Frank, Betty and Fred.
Grandmother was about sixty.

END OF AN ERA

Inval certainly was the hub of the Hutchinson Clan, but 1913 saw the death of the only two grandparents we ever knew.

Grandmother Woods died in April and on 13th June Grandfather Hutchinson died peacefully at "The Library," at the then considerable age of eighty-five. At home at Moses Hill there was a hush about the house and I asked if I might go and play with Mr Houlder's coachman's daughter. Mother, however, thought that under the circumstances it was not seemly and I was not allowed to go.

George, Jan and Christopher were recalled from Sidcot School the next day, and Father took us over to "The Library." The Oak-room downstairs had been Grandfather's bedroom for the past few months, and we sat quietly there with the curtains drawn. Presently Father walked over to the bed and drew the sheet back so that we saw Grandfather's face lying so still and white. I was not frightened though I had not quite realised what we had come for. It made a great impression on me as, of course, it was intended to do.

On the day of the funeral Hugh and I stood on the hill outside "High Inval" to watch the cortège pass by on the way to the Parish Church. Our older brothers walked in the procession but regretfully I cannot remember this occasion. So I will quote Hugh's account of it:

> "The coffin was borne on a farm wagon and was followed by a large group of very distinguished men in black, with top hats. Many of them were famous doctors and surgeons, and as the procession passed I was impressed by the thought of what a great man Grandfather must have been."

There were still the aunts both at "High Inval" and "The Library" to attract us over to Inval for many years more, and the estate became the property of Aunts Ursula and Agnes. On the death of Aunt Agnes in 1961 it passed to Laurence, and three of us, Laurence, Rachel and myself have migrated back there, though not to the original houses. A new generation is growing up there in Laurence's daughter Jane with her husband Andrew Clayton and their children, James and Elizabeth.

It is a privilege to live amid such beauty, not least with its memories of our forebears with their many gifts and steadfast outlook on life.

OVER TO INVAL

*Shottermill Pond with 'the flat and sunny hill-top' of
Marley Common in the background, circa 1880*

OF CABBAGES AND KINGS

CONCERNS CULTURE,
OUR FARMER BOY,
THE OLD ORDER CHANGETH

Two famous sayings by Mary:—

"When I grow up I want to do nothing, like Mother."

"Shakespeare – I've read all those."
        (She had read *Lambs Tales from Shakespeare*)

All in order. This photograph was taken in 1914, soon after leaving Moses Hill. Laurence arrived three years later to complete the brood.

OF CABBAGES AND KINGS

CULTURAL ACTIVITIES

I realise rather belatedly that only the briefest references have been made to *Culture*. I hope it is glimpsed here and there through the rough and tumble of my happy, carefree life in dirty boots and wet stockings; in the great woods and the cosy dark barns at Moses Hill.

Until I was twelve, when I became a day-girl at Sidcot School, I was taught at home, and the fact that I remember so little about it is because I was not interested. As I did not read till I was eight this must have caused some concern, for one holiday George was enlisted to help me. We sat side by side on the sofa and I stumbled along. At every incorrect word he said sharply "Stop." This so irritated me that I slapped his knee. Funny when one thinks of it that we both eventually became heads of schools, madly keen on Education with a capital E.

After a series of 'lady nurses' and a year or two with Miss Tateham-Jones, Father undertook the teaching of Hugh, Mary and myself in 1912. How thorough and progressive Father was in everything he undertook! He studied Froebel and Montessori and made some of the Montessori apparatus.

Hugh and Mary were clean slates so to speak, and benefited from this and learnt quickly. Mary read before she was five and was found at a bookshelf one day wondering whether to make a start on *Vanity Fair* or *Pendennis*! I do not think in fact she conquered either, but both children were devoted readers of Beatrix Potter, Hugh's favourite being 'Pigling Bland'.

Large sandpaper letters were mounted on card and Hugh would trace them with his right forefinger to learn their shapes. Arrows indicated the correct way round so that when he began to write, automatically the letters were correctly formed. We had copy-books, long since frowned upon by educationalists, but we learnt to write long-hand properly and I do not think the constant repetition did us any

141

harm. It certainly did not overtax the brain or ask anything of the imagination. One's only ambition and surely a worthy one, was to try to write each line a little better than the last. "Practice makes perfect" and other mottoes were thus instilled into us.

We also learnt to draw and I have always been grateful for this. As an architect Father was a draughtsman, as an artist he could use his knowledge of perspective and ability to draw accurately to the painting of street scenes, churches and cathedrals. These are perhaps his most successful works, though his artist's sensitivity was evident in the delicacy of his flower paintings which defy all symmetry. Sweet peas, one of the most elusive flowers to portray in watercolour was one of his favourite subjects.

In lessons we traced patterns with lovely flowing lines. We learnt to control a pencil and water colour brushes and to keep within the lines. Much of this we practised while he read History or Greek myths to us. He had a beautiful reading voice but I am afraid I enjoyed the occupation with my hands more than with my head.

There must be something wrong with me, but I took a strong dislike to Greek myths and to the cruelty of History. There was cruelty in Nature certainly. That one accepted, but much that was beautiful too. Why man had to be so cruel as to cut off poor Queen Mary's head or stretch Greeks on a bed that was in fact a rack, revolted me. There was a particularly horrid history book with coloured illustrations on every page. It was actually called "The Nursery History of England." The illustrations left nothing to the imagination. Poor Queen Mary! I can see her now, but will not describe the scene.

Geography was enjoyable. Exploration of new and exciting places with plants and animals hitherto unknown, strange coloured natives and curious dwellings. Also of course, our excursions with Father gave point to the geography of the British Isles.

Such were some of the subjects taught at stated hours round the dining-room table. But throughout this little book, as the story unfolds I hope it reveals the sowing of the seeds of culture that fell variously on different members of the family.

George, for instance, remembers with gratitude the Sunday evenings when Father showed us reproductions of Italian paintings. He was much older and more in tune with Father's intellectualism. One picture after another would come before our eyes and Father would talk simply about it. Such names as Fra Angelico, Bellini, Tintoretto, Michael Angelo and others rolled off his tongue like poetry. He would point out the delicate Italian backgrounds, and often the scenic details of these pictures appealed to me more than the over-fat babies without so much as a nappy on, when our babies were so very well covered up.

If it were not Italian Art it might well be poetry on a Sunday evening. Longfellow, Browning, Wordsworth, Tennyson; long, long sessions of them. No one dared to interrupt or stop the flow, not even Mother who got through a deal of knitting. Father more than once said that Man had achieved greater beauty than anything in Nature. I am surprised at him!

I do not think I was ever openly rebellious, but as I matured there grew within me the realisation that in the eyes of my elders and betters the study of Natural History was far inferior to that of Art, Poetry or History. Perhaps they were right. I do not know. But the result was that a barrier developed in my mind against the type of culture that was for many, many years laid on rather thick.

Curiouser and curiouser. With all this highbrow culture we were also encouraged to read little paper covered booklets sold for about a penny. There was very little of literary merit in them. They were, I suppose, for our moral awakening of the needs of others. Father would come home from London with half a dozen of such titles as *Little Meg's Children, Christy's Old Organ* and *Jessica's First Prayer*. At the age of nine and ten I wallowed in their morbid sentimentality, reading them again and again. These were children of poverty, for there were real slums in London in those days, and Little Meg was my favourite. She was the eldest of a large family and was forever nursing ailing babies and wheeling them about in rusty old prams.

Sunday evenings generally ended with hymn-singing round the piano, which Mother played. We would sing "Home, Sweet Home" ... "Be it ever so humble there's no place like home," and we meant it. We remembered the three boys at Sidcot as we sang "A Prayer for Absent Ones..."

> "Keep our loved ones now far absent
> 'Neath thy care."

and Bertel would choose "The sands of Time are sinking", a curious choice for a boy in his teens.

My favourite was, characteristically, "All things bright and beautiful" while Hugh revelled in "Onward Christian Soldiers". We would march round the room being (Quakerly!) soldiers, and then Hugh would kiss Mother and Father goodnight and be played off to bed.

Hymn singing was generally a cheerful occasion. It could also be the most emotional hour of the week, for we were normally an unemotional family not given to confidences and expected to keep a stiff upper lip. But in the middle of hymns one evening I was found to be quietly crying. Nothing would drag from me the reason. It was because our parents had been "having words" just before hymns started.

BERTEL THE FARMER BOY

I must jump sideways here to tell more about Bertel. He was not strong mentally or physically and could not cope with boarding school. Father, with a patience he seldom showed to the rest of us, taught him the elementary subjects so that he could read and write and do simple calculations. He was always happiest working with animals and during the latter part of the First World War worked on a farm where we were living near Sidcot. We still treasure the account he wrote of his work, for it is a triumph for a lad of his poor ability. This is it. (*A copy of the actual letter is reproduced on pages 147 and 148.*)

A DAY ON A FARM AT HAYMAKING

When you start on a farm in the summer, you generally start in the morning very early in the morning at 5 o'clock A.M.

We generally get up at 5 o'clock in the morning and Harness the horse in the cart and put two pails and a churn in the cart and go about 2 miles to Churchill to milk the cows in our field. We milk about five cows each then we tie the horse to the gate and wash our hands with water which we brought in the churn. Then we start milking the cows they stand quite nicely because they are used to it.

It is quite nice milking out of doors when it is fine. After we have finished milking we go to another farm to get some more milk then we go on to Winscombe. Then we have our own breakfast and after breakfast we fed the pigs. Then we went to Churchill to do some haymaking first we turned it over with the swathturner. The swathturner goes round the field the same way as the mowing machine goes. Then we have our dinner and after dinner we horse rake it up into such long rows across the field then we get staddle ready (which is the bottom of the Haymow) which consists of brambles and sticks and any sort of thing we can lay our hands on.

Bertel was happy with animals. Here he is in his Sunday best with our pony 'Kit'.

Then we start with the horse collector it takes two people to work one to lead the horse. The other to manage the haycollector. The haycollector collects the hay up and takes it up the haymow and tips over and goes off for another load and does the same with that load too. Then we drive the old grayish white mare in the milkfloat with the milk to Winscombe. I call at the same place as we did in the morning to fetch some more milk. The I feed the pigs while the milk was cooling then I took the milk to Winscombe Station then I drive back Churchill to fetch the haymakers back to Woodborough Farm Winscombe at 10.30 PM. We were glad to get back to Woodborough Farm Winscombe Somerset. We said we have had a nice day of Haymaking. I rode back to Winscombe on our greyish mare. It was a nice ride from Churchill Somersetshire.

Goodnight.

(Signed)

HODGE.

The signature is, of course, Bertel's little joke, for Hodge denotes a farmer and there is a theory that the name Hutchinson is derived from Hodge's son.

In the autumn of 1918 a severe form of influenza swept through the country and Bertel succumbed. Pneumonia set in and he died a few weeks before the war ended. He was twenty. His poor frame was worn out in service to his country as a farm labourer, working cheerfully up to eighteen hours a day on his clumsy, ill-formed feet. We sang his hymn at his funeral at the Friends' Meeting House at Sidcot and Father carved an oak headstone on his grave. This has recently been replaced by a stone.

Black Beauty had been Bertel's favourite story which he had read again and again. Father cherished also a tattered little volume *Farming Shown to Children.* How fortunate for this simple brother of ours that his childhood had been spent in the freedom of Moses Hill Farm where our lives were our own and amusements were of our own unsophisticated making. Where also we mixed with country folk like the Wheelers, Edgar Head and George Parvin.

A, D A Y, ON, A FARM.

AT HAYMAKING

When you start on a farm in the summer you generally start in the morning very early in the morning at 5 oclock A.M.

We generally get up at 5 oclock in the morning and Harness the horse in the cart and put two pail and a churn in the cart and go about 2 mills to Churchill to milk ten cows in our field we milk about five cows each then we tie the horse to the gate and wash our hands with water which we brought in the churn, Then we start milking the cows they stand quite nicely because they are used to it. It is quite nice milking out of doors when it is fine. After we have finished milking we go to another farm to get some more milk then we go on to Winscomb There we have our breakfast and after breakfast we bed the pigs. Then we went to churchill to do some haymaking first we turned it over with the swathturner, the swathturner goes round the field the same way as the mowing machine goes Then we have our dinner and after dinner we horse rake it up into such long rows across the field then we staddle ready (which is the bottom of the Haymow) which consists of brambles and sticks and any sort of thing we can lay our hands on. Then we start with the horse collector it takes two people to work one to lead the

147

horse The other to mange the haycollector. The Haycollector collects the hay up and takes it up to the haymow and tips over and goes off for another load and does the same with that load too. Then we go and milk the cows at churchill then I drive the old greyish white mare in the milkfloat with the milk to Winscombe I call at the same place as we did in the morning to fetch some more milk The I feed the pigs while the milk was cooling then I took the milk to Winscombe Station then I drive back Churchill the to fetch the haymakers to back to Woodborough Farm Winscombe at 10.31 P.M. We were glad to get back to Woodborough Farm Winscombe somerset we said we have had a nice day of Haymaking. I rode back to Winscombe on our greyish mare it was a nice ride from Churchill Somerset.
GoodNight.

———————

Signed
Hodge

Bertel's Day on a Farm – the original letter

A MILESTONE – 1913

Now to the year 1913. I was old enough now to remember more clearly what our home looked like, for it too had a cultural influence upon us. The living rooms had pictures on the walls, many of them. Some by local artists, Josiah Whymper and his son Charles, some by Father himself and reproductions of Old Masters. There was a tendency in wall-papers, curtains, etc, towards the William Morris style, much in fashion just then. On the mantel shelves carved by Father's own hands, were ornaments, not too many and not pretentious. Vases and bowls brought back from holidays in Brittany and Italy, but never, oh never, the cheap "Present from Brighton" type of thing. Two brass candlesticks, one taller than the other, were probably picked up cheap because they were not a pair. I treasure them still.

There was also an angel in white china that I loved dearly, kneeling, gazing into a bowl which Mother and I filled with primroses each spring. But the pièce de resistance was the cuckoo clock. It had been a wedding present from Uncle Llewellyn, Father's brother, and all my life has cheered me on with its cheerful cuckoo-ing every half hour. It has been the joy and wonder of countless small children and long may it continue.

China used at table must have been broken and replaced many times and there were some oddments that amused us. Christopher has cause to remember the butter dish with the motto round the edge "Dinna let yer modesty wrang ye," for he took this excellent advice only to be accused by Mother of being greedy. The bread board has been in daily use for eighty-five years. It too was a wedding present, and the prayer carved around it has almost disappeared. It reads of course "Give us this day our daily bread." The mind boggles at the thought of the number of loaves that have been sliced on it.

There *was* a silver tea-pot but that was pawned (well, not literally) to pay for our education.

Yes, 1913. Our newest baby Elizabeth Rachel arrived in March; soon after, Grandmother Woods and then Grandfather Hutchinson died, but the summer wore on happily enough for innocent children. There was no radio or T.V. to introduce us prematurely to the world of adult greed and political intrigue. We were too busy about our own small interests to feel doubts or shadows cast from outside our little world.

Were we too sheltered? I do not think so. History was ever placed before us. Father spoke of wars and heroes, of attempts on our islands bravely repulsed (since 1066, of course), of Rule Britannia, and the might of our Empire (all those red patches on the map of the world), and of the downfall of wicked aggressors typified at that time by Napoleon Bonaparte.

Did he wonder, however, if civilisation was getting a bit out of hand, for he was apt to be rather scornful of some modern trends such as extravagance and glorification for its own sake. The sinking of the *Titanic* the year before had filled us all with shocked interest. It was the largest ship afloat and much admired for its luxurious comfort. On its maiden voyage across the Atlantic it struck an iceberg and sank with the loss of over twelve hundred lives, more than half its full complement. It was a calamity that shook the country by its enormity.

In the same year (1912) had come the tragic end of Scott's attempt to be first to reach the South Pole. Though saddened, Father, ever a cautious man himself, had little sympathy with those who risked their lives to be first anywhere. He had known Edward Whymper of Matterhorn fame, personally but thought more of his father and brother, the artists.

Only three years after the *Titanic* disaster the *Lusitania* went down. This was the result of enemy action for we were then at war with Germany. There was personal interest in this too, for a distant relation, Foster Stackhouse, was one who was drowned. He was a friend of Scott and had wanted George to join a team on an Antarctic expedition. Father would not countenance such waste of time and talent. We all heard about *that*.

Did Father's caution and insistence on the importance of intellectual advancement, and also his very sincere feeling of responsibility for his family, colour the outlook of his children? I can only speak for myself. It did.

He spoke much about evolution also, applying it to man as an evolving of all things true and beautiful. Following his father he taught us that Heaven was here on earth if we could make it so; that our aim should be to leave behind us at the end of life something a little better for our being there. He hoped to do this through his children. A solemn thought, but a challenge.

Both parents were very loyal subjects of the Crown, seeing in it a stability lacking in other heads of state. They had taken George at the age of three and three-quarters to Southsea beach on a cold January day to watch the funeral cortège of Queen Victoria as it came across the Spithead from Osborne in the Isle of Wight. The German Kaiser was in a white yacht, Mother often told us. It stood out against the black and grey of the other ships, as he intended it should.

OF CABBAGES AND KINGS

When King Edward VII came to open the Midhurst Sanatorium in 1906 Mother marshalled her brood, of which I was then the youngest, up on a bank on the corner of the drive. "Mind that child doesn't fall," said an interfering woman standing by. Mother was incensed. She would see that her child did not fall. She would also make sure that the child saw the King. I was only two and a half.

Kings, queens, emperors. By 1913, I wonder if a cloud was looming up on the horizon of those parents of ours? Father would certainly be wondering as he read the paper if Kaiser William had any nefarious intentions. "The Prussians are conceited, aggressive people," he told us. Both parents might well be thinking of their growing boys, for George was leaving school in a year's time.

In the meanwhile, with eight children Moses Hill was bursting at the seams. Just down the hill a much larger house stood empty. The inevitable happened. On 14th October as we finished breakfast Father announced calmly, "We are moving down to Kingsley Dene today. Take the pictures off the walls and carry them down."

All day we toiled up and down the Hollow carrying pictures under our arms, and anything else we could manage. Mr Wheeler went back and forth via The Gully with the farm cart. The only one who did nothing to help was Rachel. She was only six months old and lay crying on a mattress in our new nursery that evening.

"Never mind, Missy, I'll bring your cot down the very next load," said kind old Tom Wheeler.

Our life at Moses Hill had ended.

'October House', previously 'Yafflesmead',
shortly before it was demolished in 2003

RECOLLECTIONS OF KINGSLEY GREEN

Previous chapters dealt with my life at Moses Hill Farm
up to 1913 and mentions at the end that we moved
down the hill to the lovely house, Kingsley Dene.
These recollections carry on from there.

"Our Shop" in Kingsley Green, 1960

RECOLLECTIONS OF KINGSLEY GREEN

REGIMENTS AND REFUGEES

Living at Kingsley Green during the First World War when I was aged ten plus, broadened my hitherto limited horizons. A regiment of Gordon Highlanders was stationed at Fernhurst and we had two officers billeted on us. One was a well-educated young New Zealander, Lieutenant Roberton, who joked with us. I remember him being offered an orange. "No thank you" he said, "but I enjoy hearing Hugh eating his." Hugh was my young brother. He was sucking noisily at an orange with a hole in it plugged with a lump of sugar. Very yum-yum. Lieutenant Husky was a braw Scot almost un-understandable to Southerners such as us.

Kilts! Sporrans! The servants conjectured in whispers as to what was worn, if anything, beneath them. On Sundays our nurse, Phoebe Wheeler, took us down to Fernhurst Cross to watch the parade. Kilts swayed rhythmically to the skirl of bagpipes as the Highlanders marched and counter-marched before the admiring crowd of villagers. I wonder if anyone there had ever seen the like before. Few country folk travelled far in those days and there was no TV to bring such displays into our homes. I begged Mother for a kilt. With such a large family to clothe it was not fair to use so much material on one little girl, so she made me a plaid frock instead: not at all the same thing.

The Highlanders departed. Belgium was being overrun by the Germans and refugees poured over to London. Father went up three times and returned with Belgian families to share our safe country retreat. The first consisted of Monsieur and Madame Hardy, their town children, Hermann and Elsa, and Madame's parents. They were charming people who spoke excellent French. We swapped phrases of each other's languages. "Tout-les-deux" meant "both". One day when

155

there were three puddings at dinner – probably bits to finish up from the previous day – Hermann asked his mother what the English for "Tout les trois" was. My mother was very amused, his own maman rather embarrassed. He was given all three, for Mother liked to see her puddings appreciated.

Monsieur Hardy was a director of the tramways in Antwerp and soon he and his father-in-law returned and, finding the occupation tenable, sent for the women and children to join them.

Next, Father came home with an elderly couple and their delicate grown-up son. They cooked for themselves and lived separately from us, the son complaining that his mother cooked "Toujours semole." It became a sort of lament. "Toujours semole", 'always semolina.' This young man taught us French and I made good progress, so that when I went to secondary school it was said I spoke like a Frenchman. Alas, I lost it all. The teaching was dull and I was poor at the written word and did not try. I am left with a French accent and no words to put it to!

The Stappers also returned to their homeland and the next arrivals came one wet, windy evening in October. I never knew how many, they did not stay for long enough to be counted. They were the family housed in "The Chalet", (later known as 'Tamalpais') and terrified by the night time fall of chestnuts.

SELF SUFFICIENCY

Perhaps after that Father thought he had done enough. He concentrated on feeding his own family, growing all manner of fruit and vegetables. He did this with great perseverance and success throughout two world wars. Apples from the orchard were stored on the floor of an attic, along with those barrow-loads of sweet chestnuts – we would not go short of food if Father had anything to do with it.

Mother too, was determined we should not starve and, in season, took us blackberrying along the hedgerows and whortleberrying on Marley and Blackdown. Mushrooms were gathered and young nettle leaves served as "spinach" once or twice, but were not appreciated. Of course there were hens, and Father tried keeping rabbits. They bred like the proverbials, but got some fatal disease and "died like flies". Many's the funeral enjoyed by us children under the fir trees. We tolled the bell (a tin with a nail in it hung high in a tree), dug little graves and picked posies of wildflowers. On one occasion the cortege had to be halted while the corpse finished dying. What little ghouls country children are!

In 1916 we departed to live in Somerset to be near enough to the school we patronised, to be able to attend as day scholars. How homesick we were for Sussex. Somerset was so relaxing, we always felt sleepy. So in 1923 we moved back, this time to a new house, Yafflesmead, built in part by Father's and my own older brothers' own hands. The carved oak staircase and carved overmantles were Father's work. He showed me how to carve and I was entrusted to do some of the simpler work.

OF SCOUTS AND SCHOOLS

My brothers were now hooked on Scouting and I took up Cubs. My first assignment was as assistant Cubmaster to Mr Lawson, the Lay Reader at Fernhurst. I don't remember very much about this except that the cubs' jerseys had all been hand-knitted by some kind ladies and were handed down and down until they really were not very smart. We never seemed to have any money to spend and Mr Lawson was always saying that it was "the spirit that counts, not the letter" and we remained shabby.

A Scout and Cub Rally was held at Ropes, the home of Sir Arthur and Lady Balfour. Her Ladyship was a great patron of Scouting. A visiting troop was camping nearby and was invited to the rally. A marquee was erected for the boys' tea and scouters were divided between the drawing-room and the kitchen. Mr Lawson qualified for the drawing-room, our Scoutmaster, a gardener, departed happily to the kitchen. I said firmly that I must stay with the boys to see that they behaved. There was great consternation however, when a horrified Mr Lawson hurried out to whisper to me that the visiting Scoutmaster had been sent to the kitchen. He was a vicar in disguise! There was nothing I could do but laugh. No doubt the bread-and-butter was more filling out there!

Later, I became Cubmaster at Camelsdale where two of my brothers, Jan and Hugh, were in succession, Scoutmasters. We had some marvellous camps, twice at St. Helens in the Isle of Wight. We set off laden with large fruit cakes made for us by the boys' mothers and quantities of vegetables freshly dug from their fathers' gardens.

A boy one day had been very disobedient and was sent to his tent in disgrace. The trouble with tents is that you can't shut the door. He disappeared for several hours. At dusk I was pacing the sea shore imagining I could see a body floating in the sea. But at cocoa time he emerged from a nearby wood feeling hungry. I am afraid he was packed off home the next day, and Hugh, who met him at Haslemere station, reported that he looked as if he had travelled under the seat.

As Cub Commissioner for the Midhurst District I enjoyed visiting packs in many Sussex villages during the winter evenings, and running district camps at Marley in the summer.

By now I had my own car. In 1929 I was left £100 by an aunt with which I bought a second-hand Rover 10 HP. Hugh often shared the driving when he was at home. What fun we had travelling about the countryside. We didn't mind a bit that the plugs were often oiling up. We unscrewed them, burnt off the oil with a match and all was well. One day however I called in at Green's Garage in Haslemere and said to the boy who came out to attend to me "I think a plug is 'missing'. Would you please look". He opened the bonnet and peered inside. "They're all there Miss, four", he assured me.

Margaret Hutchinson with children at her Yafflesmead school
in July 1939

I was now a trained teacher with some experience of teaching in Haslemere. Being an independent soul eager to put into practice the Froebelian principles learned at College, I decided to open my Froebel Kindergarten school. My brothers and sisters were seldom at home and my parents agreed to let me have several rooms in our capacious house. The car was a valuable asset in getting the school established.

After school was over each day six or seven small children were packed in, two at least on the front seat, and I ferried them home to Haslemere via Camelsdale and Shottermill.

There was another Miss Hutchinson, in Haslemere, no relation, with a little school. She thought we should do better to combine, and wrote to me: "You have the car, I have the children", but I did not respond. Presently the school grew too big for the car to be of much help and we relied on buses. More families had cars also, though not more than one per household, for a long while to come.

WARTIME AGAIN

Then came World War Two. When hostilities really seemed imminent advertising appeared in the daily papers asking for accommodation in country areas for people living in London. So it was that two elderly widows in black arrived at our house by taxi. Their trunks were carried up to our large spare bedroom which they proceeded to share for the next four years. They were very London but managed to accept our country style without complaining. Each morning after washing up (they certainly did their bit at the kitchen sink) they crept silently into the living-room, one with a mop, the other a duster and did the daily. Then, donning hats and coats they sallied forth to our one and only shop "Mills", about ten minutes away at their speed. The afternoon was spent in their bedroom from which they emerged at tea-time. Between tea and supper they occupied the two armchairs by the fire, Mrs A. knitting, Mrs C. endlessly darning her combinations until they were a wonderful patchwork of neat rectangular darns. After supper they retired upstairs for the night while my parents eased their weary bodies into the same armchairs.

This was the routine for four long years, yet when at last it ended we slipped back into pre-war family life without giving them a thought!

During the bad air raids on the coastal towns two other elderly ladies whom we knew, joined us from Hastings. Presently they found rooms in Haslemere.

Food rationing was much more organised than in the first war. Even hens were rationed. Mother had always kept hens: now we could only buy enough chicken-food for one hen per ration book. When there were five people in the house, we had five hens. Mother had to think of names for them. She named them after five sisters, distant cousins of ours, in New Zealand: Belle, Nell, Bess, Fan, Edith. As they ceased to be steady layers they were in turn put in the pot. "We are eating Bess today" Mother would remind us. There was an unfortunate reaction to this in 1961 when I visited relations in N.Z. I told them this story and they were not amused. Belle, Nell, Bess, Fan, Edith were their revered aunts not so long deceased. I had to play on the half-truth that in Britain life had been very, very hard and we were extremely short of protein. They had mutton galore!

Any supplement to a meat ration was more than welcome. Or almost any. We did manage to dissuade Mother from cooking up a squirrel that had been shot. She had heard, I think through the Women's Institute, that squirrel tasted like chicken, but we were not convinced. It went into the pot for the hens however. Waste not want not.

FOOD AND FORMS

Father still dug the garden, leaning more and more heavily on the spade as he became more arthritic, but never giving in. One year we picked two hundred pounds of gooseberries. They helped greatly with school dinners. Three days a week we gave dinners to about thirty children. For this we had a canteen licence for children and helpers. We were able to include our old ladies and ourselves as everyone had some job to do. Mother was in charge of cooking and was helped by a rota of school mums, all anxious for these extra meals beyond their rations. There were the inevitable forms to fill in and one day I was given a really terrific dressing-down by the food controller in Midhurst for being late in sending in these stupid forms. A man was standing just behind me, awaiting his turn. "Never mind", he said quietly as, crestfallen, I turned to go, "the war will end one day".

Red tape and elaborate form filling was always anathema to me, and I felt in wartime one had more important things to do. The school children had milk each morning. It came in third of a pint bottles. Sometimes a child would be absent. I was told categorically that members of staff were not to have this milk. It must be poured down the sink. Well, if Miss Bayliss's bicycle basket served as a sink, so be it. She was delighted to take home a third of a pint of milk. I can still see the look of gratitude on her face!

When I wasn't teaching in the afternoons I dug my own patch of vegetables, either selling them to Harold Mills at the shop, in aid of the Red Cross, or else sending them off in the car that passed by once a week collecting up produce for the sailors at Portsmouth. There was a shed on Chilcroft Road where we collected waste paper and books and once a week I took my turn at sorting and packing. We sent books, including music, to a camp of German and Austrian internees near Liverpool. They had been put into a new, even unfinished, housing estate, with the barest of furniture and nothing to do. Many were highly intellectual men who had fled from the Nazi domination. Several of their children came to my school. One was a "baby baron", the others children of University professors. Gradually their fathers were released and some emigrated to America.

THROUGH THE WOODS

The war brought many more children to school despite the difficulty of getting petrol. They piled into the bus from Haslemere, and others walked. There were always a few from the Blackdown area, trotting along woodland paths clutching the first primroses and bluebells; dropping shoes on the way home as they enjoyed the freedom of running barefoot once they were away from adult supervision.

A little bevy from Fernhurst, the Blockeys and the Warrens amongst them, were seen off home each afternoon to walk through the woods. They loved this. But one day Mrs Warren went in search as they had not turned up on time. She found them huddled under a tree having scared each other almost to the point of paralysis with gruesome stories of ghosts, wolves etc – all purely imaginative.

Talking of the woods: I had one summer erected a hide, like a very small tent, beside a willow warbler's nest near Vann Common, intending to watch the birds from it. But someone reported it to the police at Fernhurst who took it away. I had to go and claim it from the police station. It shows the state of dithers that people could get into at that time. My poor little tent was only a faded old curtain with tropical forest and monkeys printed on it. Who could have thought it was German!

Hitler did pay calls on us a few times. On one occasion a German bomber cruised along so low that the swastika was plainly visible. He sent his envoy one night when my brother Laurence was home on leave, and dropped a bomb so near that it sounded as if it was beside the drive. It scrunched down but did not explode. The next morning school was cancelled while my assistant teacher and I looked for it. We found it further down the wood where it had made a deep hole in the clay. A little girl, daughter of a doctor, was seen at large in Haslemere that morning and was asked why she was not at school. "They've got an expectant bomb there" she replied. Haslemere was full of unexploded mums evacuated from London at the time, and her mother was busy trying to cope with them. (Hush! We never talked like this before the war. Never!)

The Battle of Britain in the summer of 1940 was unforgettable. There was a continuous buzz very high up in the blue sky; so high that the planes looked like insects. It was hard to believe that they contained men. The little boys raced about the playground bombing and shooting. One said pointing upwards "I'd love to hit it." "There are men inside it, you know", I replied. He stopped suddenly, "I hadn't thought of that", he said soberly. After hostilities ended in 1945 and we were collecting up tins of food to drop into starving Holland, the same little boys raced round dropping imaginary food parcels instead of bombs.

OUR SHOP

I cannot leave the war years without mention of our shop. Since the death of Mr Ebenezer Mills, it had been run by his son Harold. Little had changed over the years and bacon rashers were still cut on a hand-operated circular saw. There was not the wide choice of groceries we expect now but what we got was very good. Harold looked after our needs throughout the war most capably, dealing with ration books, "points" and the occasional off-the-ration perks as fairly as was humanly possible. He was magnificent!

There being no other communal meeting place at Kingsley Green, gossip was exchanged in this tiny shop and it is one of my lasting regrets that I did not write down at the time some of the drama that went on there; the friendships made, the jokes told, the rejoicings and the sorrows shared. And all the while Harold was serving customers at full speed, scribbling down their purchases in a large day-book in his unique short-hand. From this every now and then he would copy out every item and its price into one's order book and tot up pages of small amounts: he would then send it in. It might be months coming! Trust abounded.

THE BAKER

The bakery adjoined the shop and Harold's brother Jack did the baking very early in the morning before milking the cows, for there was a small farm also.

Baking was done in the old country oven built into the wall and heated by faggots, just as it had been in my childhood. There was always a large stack of these bundles of twiggy wood standing outside the back of the bakery. Mills' bread was well-liked and they had a very wide delivery round. Often they were delivering late into the evening.

Before the war delivery was done by horse and cart; after, when Harold's son David was demobbed from the army, he drove a small van. Bread and groceries were brought right into our kitchen, and meat was still ordered and delivered from Haslemere. We had been on the telephone at Yafflesmead since some time in the 1920's and found it invaluable.

It is curious to reflect that in those days we always ate white bread; lovely crispy white loaves. There was much grumbling in the war that the flour was not so white. It took on a greyish colour and we were told it was fortified with something or other and was good for us. There was talk of "vitamins" and "roughage". "What are all these vitamins?" my father exclaimed scornfully, "We did perfectly well without them."

I am convinced that two things in particular kept us healthy in the war, our simple uncluttered ration was supplemented by fresh fruit and vegetables, and we were too busy to be ill.

POST-WAR LIFE

Food and clothing rationing continued sometime after 1945 but gradually we settled down to peace-time routine once more. When oranges first came in, a small boy, on being given one, bit straight into it. There was a shout of "Not like that! Peel it!" He was so embarrassed that he pretended to like it that way and ate it all. Bananas were sold for children and old people only, but some youngsters thought they were horrid.

In 1947 we had one of the rare freeze-ups when snow lay on the ground for at least two months. Uncleared roads became icy ruts. There was a silver thaw caused by rain falling and freezing immediately so that everything from a blade of grass to tree trunks, branches and twigs were coated in ice. It was a truly wonderful sight, especially on a bright moonlit night. The woods glistened and tinkled. It was like living in a glass world. The roads were terribly slippery and yet one had to go out and experience it.

I took the children up the hill to Marley Heights. Bushes were bowed over and the children crept up inside the fairy-like ice caverns. Mr Frederick Goldring had walked up from Timberscombe with his camera. One of his photographs was reproduced in the book "The Weald" by S.W. Wooldridge, in The New Naturalist series.

I have only known a silver thaw twice in my life. The second time was in 1963 when we again had a two month freeze-up.

A most glorious summer followed but many of the children fell ill with measles. A high temperature in the very hot weather pulled them down and when they returned to school they looked very wan indeed. We went easy on lessons but enjoyed making raffia mats and baskets; a pleasant repetitive occupation with a rewarding result.

'Silver Thaw' on trees, 1st March 1947

NATURAL HISTORY EDUCATION

The school always had a keenness for Natural History and there are many stories I could tell of our first-hand experiences. There was the brimstone butterfly that we followed into the wood and watched lay an egg on a leaf of alder buckthorn. We took the twig back to the classroom and reared the butterfly right through till we were able to let it fly away. This took most of the summer term.

There was the spider that obligingly spun its web from a boy's outstretched arm while the whole class watched its every move. There was the extraordinary occurrence of Susan Warren's budgerigar. Susan arrived at school one day almost in tears. Her budgie had escaped and was lost. In the middle of the morning my Mother came to say that a budgie was in her bedroom. Sure enough it was Susan's! It must have followed the car all along Vann Lane, up Friday's Hill, round the corner by Kingsley Green and so to Yafflesmead. Or did it fly over the wood, at least a mile, and arrive by chance at our house? Anyway, all ended well.

The two Pallant sisters walked daily from their home near Blackdown, often bringing us interesting nature news. One morning I found two baby brown owls in a basket on my desk. They had fallen from their nest and Mrs Pallant had apparently said "Take them to school and I don't want them back." We managed to rear them in spite of stringent meat rationing in operation at the time. Even offal was hard to come by. The children brought rats

'Tootles' the owl
(from "Children as Naturalists")

and mice, robbing their cats to feed our owls. We called them Peter and Wendy, the lost children. They were very tame and obliged many an audience by showing off how they could swallow mice whole.

In the summer holidays they grew up sufficiently to take

themselves off into the woods. The next year we were asked to take another young owl that had been found abandoned. This was Tootles, and was a great success. He was so friendly that after he was liberated he would fly home at dusk if I called, and settle on my hand.

These and many other natural history exploits were described in my book "Children as Naturalists", now out of print but which was used in Teacher Training colleges for some years. The opportunities for first-hand experiences were much greater thirty years ago than now. Children were much freer to wander alone, and flowers and birds were much more abundant. One never had to say "don't pick" this or that, unless it was a really rare plant.

Curiously, however, there were very few Roe deer in the woods and they never came into the garden although it was quite unfenced. Rabbits were a pest before myxomatosis. Magpies were uncommon. Our garden at the edge of the wood had four kinds of warblers nesting as well as finches, thrushes and tits of several species.

I would erect small hides from which the children took turns to watch young birds being fed in their nests at a distance of a few feet. The drill was that one child escorted another to the hide and when he was settled in it, walked away. The birds, being unable to count, thought the coast was clear and returned to the nest with food for the young. The child in the hide must not come out until fetched; that would spoil the deception.

One day we heard that the Queen Mother was to visit the King Edward VII Hospital at Midhurst, so we tidied ourselves up and set off up to the main road to wave to her as she passed. Running along the path we heard someone calling loudly. We had forgotten Clive! He was in the hide by the treecreepers' nest. He was hastily rescued and joined the party.

We waited at the roadside near The Guest House (later Otara Nursing Home). A corgi dog which seemed to have the freedom of Kingsley Green joined us. Soon a police car came along, its loud hailer telling us to keep to the side please, and then the royal car approached. The corgi chose this moment to cross the road. "How awful", I thought "She'll think it's my dog!" But as the car slowed up the Queen leaned out and smiled at the impudent little dog.

AND SO TO INVAL

My school was becoming rather burdensome as my parents grew older and more frail and in need of my care. They had been so very kind and helpful, and tolerant of the many little people about, sometimes as many as fifty in the house. So I let the school wind down till in 1956 it finally closed. It had a run of 25 years.

It is difficult to know where to end one's recollections of old times. 1957 when my father died at almost 89 seems but yesterday to me but there are adults today who may read this, who were not even thought of then. My memories of Kingsley Green end in 1958 however, when we sold Yafflesmead. It had been a very lovely home and school, variously described by visitors as "fairyland" and "paradisiacal". But Mother and I now felt the draught and were glad to accept my brother Laurence's very kind offer of a snug little "Granny Grace" on the end of his house at Inval, close by the house where Mother had spent her childhood some eighty years earlier.

Margaret Hutchinson 'dressed up' for a party in 1988

POSTSCRIPT

Margaret Massey Hutchinson (MMH)
1904–1997

by Penny Hollow

A NATURALIST REMEMBERED

I first met Margaret Hutchinson in the early 1970s, when I was a young trainee at Haslemere Educational Museum. Following in the footsteps of her aunt, Agnes Hutchinson, she was much involved with the Museum (which had been founded by her grandfather), as an active committee member, Honorary Librarian and trustee. A tall and imposing figure, she was greatly respected and everyone at the Museum was slightly in awe of her, always ensuring that her requests (polite notes signed with the characteristic "MMH") were quickly acted upon.

LIFE "UPSTAIRS"

One day in 1978, I had a totally unexpected phone call from her. She had heard that I was in a rather cramped bed-sit – would I like to go and live "upstairs" in her house at Inval? Some years earlier arthritis had forced her to adapt to ground floor living and "upstairs" had become a small flat that she rented out to carefully chosen tenants. Without hesitation I accepted and there followed eight idyllic years at the Croft House, high on that secluded hillside above Haslemere.

MMH was never anything like a typical landlady and to me, as to many other young people, she became a friend and much-respected mentor. It was a household where a passion for natural history was the expected norm and where the comings and goings of the natural world were at least as important as the doings of friends and neighbours. I would return home each evening with keen anticipation, knowing that there might be news to hear of a local wren's nest or a freshly dissected plant gall to view under the microscope.

As arthritis curtailed her walks I was privileged to act as her scout, tramping the local woods and fields in search of specimens for her gall research and sightings for her monthly Nature Notes column. On fine summer evenings I would be despatched to count glow-worms at the bottom of the garden or to watch bats over the Moat. However, she did not allow disability to restrict her travels entirely and she would set off down muddy and rutted woodland tracks in her elderly Hillman, a vehicle certainly never designed for off-road use, whose gears had a will of their own. A kindly guardian angel must have been around, as she always returned safely.

MMH valued her independence and although she was happy to delegate small errands to her friends, she preferred assistance with finding, or making, simple gadgets to solve problems. My favourite project was the design of a combined dustbin-lid-lifter-and-badger-baffle. MMH found the heavy metal dustbin lid difficult to manage whilst using walking sticks, but the local badger had no difficulty in tipping it off with an almighty crash at midnight. A careful arrangement of cords and a counterweight solved this problem, allowing the lid to be lifted with one finger, but giving any marauding badger a salutary (but non-injurious) biff on the snout.

A SUCCESSFUL AUTHOR

During those years she was generally writing something, either her column for the local newspaper or a piece for a natural history journal. Soon, however, she was quietly working on the story of her childhood, neatly hand-written with a biro, as she never took to a typewriter. In mid 1981, after weeks of patient proof reading, the first edition of "A Childhood in Edwardian Sussex" arrived from the publishers. That evening, not even the insistent clamour of the cuckoo clock could recall me to my forgotten supper as I read the book from cover to cover.

The first edition was quickly out of print, its success surprising and delighting the author. With advice (not always welcomed), from the publisher, she made minor modifications for the second (1983) edition including a full colour cover to replace her own line drawings. That also sold steadily and when it in turn was out of print, copies were eagerly sought in second-hand bookshops.

MMH was able to stay in her own home until the last few weeks before her death in July 1997. She continued researching and writing until her sight deteriorated and she ensured that her plant gall collection was carefully indexed before she donated it to Haslemere Museum.

After her death I was asked to write an article on her natural history connections for the local paper and, with the help of her friends and after much enjoyable browsing amongst her notes and scrapbooks, I was able to compile a portrait of a dedicated naturalist.

NATURALIST AND TEACHER

Margaret Hutchinson was a member of Haslemere Natural History Society for 74 years, surely a record. In 1978 she was elected an Honorary Member in recognition of her support as a committee member, keen field worker, leader and writer and, in more recent years, by maintaining the local bird records.

Her deep interest in natural history, and particularly birds, had begun in childhood and at the age of twelve she had submitted a detailed and beautifully illustrated essay on local birds to her school Junior Nature Society. (The original is now at Haslemere Museum, together with her notebooks and fascinating journals, written over nearly 80 years.)

Writing in 1989 for the Journal of the British Plant Gall Society, she said "At the Quaker School, Sidcot, in Somerset, I made no mark beyond being on the committee of the Natural History Society and writing the bird reports of our annual outing to Brean Down." Despite this modesty she had undoubtedly absorbed a wide range of knowledge, for she was a successful teacher. From 1931 to 1955 she provided a sound and imaginative education for dozens of children. "Professionally I was a Froebel trained teacher with my own school hidden in the woods near Haslemere. Here were endless opportunities for Nature Study with young children: tracking in the snow, watching nesting birds from hides, collecting wild flowers, rearing butterflies. Nature-wise we were always on tip-toe."

MMH had endless patience with the children, but less with some of the teachers she met. "My school 'Yafflesmead' closed in 1955 as I had to care for my ageing parents, but I wrote several books for children and did some lecturing and holiday courses for teachers. I could have wept at the ignorance I met. Instance the teacher who gazed sentimentally down on a grass-grown ant-hill and remarked 'To think one ant can make all that'."

FRIENDS AND COLLEAGUES

MMH often said that nature study was best enjoyed alone or with a single companion. For many years that companion was another local naturalist, Phyllis Bond. In pre-war days, they would stay in a railway Camping Coach at Pagham, where they would spend all the daylight hours bird-watching and plant hunting along the shores of the Harbour.

Although MMH took her studies very seriously, she had a keen sense of fun, never more obvious than in 1988 when she appeared at the Natural History Society's Centenary garden party at Shulbrede Priory, unrecognisably attired as a dour Victorian farm labourer. Arthur Jewell, former Museum curator, remembered an earlier occasion:

"It must have been in 1949 when I first met MMH, at her unique little school, Yafflesmead. One fine summer's day I attended an open-air performance of 'Hiawatha' which took place on the lawn. The main house was the family home and there was an additional wooden classroom situated in the extensive grounds. As the play proceeded there was a loud noise of "WHOOOO" and from the shrubbery adjoining the lawn emerged the extraordinary figure of Margaret Hutchinson, draped in old hessian sacking, in her role of *The North Wind.* The children seemed startled and I was astonished!"

John Puttick, himself a retired teacher and keen naturalist, continued: "Between friends Margaret was most often affectionately referred to by her initials, "M.M." She and I co-operated in arranging an exhibition of children's work on their interests in natural history, at the Museum. She was most critical of any indication that undue adult help had been involved: it was the young effort that was sought to be encouraged and rewarded.

"In 1988, the Natural History Society's centenary, I asked her if she would write the foreword to the booklet – "The First Century" – which celebrated the event. She kindly agreed and we went through the text together. She was highly critical of any error, not merely in grammatical nicety but in the exact choice of word to suit the statement. She kept handy Roget's Thesaurus to resolve any difficulty."

In her 60s she took up a new hobby, the study of plant galls (particularly those caused by insects) and within ten years had become a well-known and respected expert. As a teacher she had enjoyed sharing and passing on her interests, but she felt that this had kept her at a fairly elementary level. Now she wished, for her own satisfaction, to try to add a little to scientific knowledge. Laura Ponsonby, herself an accomplished botanist, recalled:

"M.M. inspired everyone to start looking at these curious structures. She made a systematic study of galls – "sleeving" them and maintaining a reference collection (now housed at Haslemere Museum). She discovered a new gall, the Kola (or Cola-nut) Gall and corresponded with other enthusiasts throughout Britain and abroad.

"In latter years I used to go to tea with her, when she could no longer get about and could hardly see. The conversation was very lively and ranged over many topics, from galls, glow-worms and gardening to matters of social or scientific interest. Her standards never slipped and an excellent tea was provided."

She was a remarkable, able and ardent naturalist, always willing to draw on the immense knowledge she acquired through her abiding interest in every aspect of the countryside. It was this knowledge she used to delight readers of the "Haslemere Herald" with the Museum Nature Notes, which she wrote for over 20 years.

MMH's naturalist friends remember her with respect and much affection. She was always interested in what one had to say and listened with great attention. Her enthusiasm and constructive comments were encouraging and she inspired many younger friends with the confidence to take their hobbies seriously. Without any doubt, she had risen to the challenge that her father had set her. It was a great privilege to know her.

Other books of Local Interest

೧ഹ ೧ഹ ೧ഹ

*Heatherley—by Flora Thompson—her sequel to the 'Lark Rise'
trilogy.* This is the book which Flora Thompson wrote about her time
in the area where the counties of Hampshire, Surrey and Sussex meet.
It is the 'missing' fourth part to her *Lark Rise to Candleford* in which
'Laura Goes Further.' Full of interest to those who know this area.
Illustrated with chapter-heading line drawings by Hester Whittle.
Introduction by Ann Mallinson.
ISBN 1-873855-29-X Sept 1998, paperback, 178pp, incl. maps.

*The Hilltop Writers—a Victorian Colony among the Surrey Hills, by
W.R. Trotter.* Rich in detail yet thoroughly readable, this book tells of
sixty-six writers including Tennyson, Conan Doyle and Bernard Shaw
who chose to work among the hills around Haslemere and Hindhead in
the last decades of the 19th century.
*ISBN 1-873855-31-1 March 2003, paperback, 260pp, illustrations
plus maps.*

Shottermill—its Farms, Families and Mills, by Greta Turner.
A comprehensive history of the area surrounding the point where the
counties of Hampshire, Surrey and Sussex meet, including a
description of the mill-based industries supported there by the presence
of the southern River Wey.
Part 1—Early Times to the 1700s *ISBN 1-873855-39-7*
Part 2—1700s to the present day *ISBN 1-873855-40-0*
Illustrations plus maps. To be published late 2003 & 2004.

The Southern Wey—a guide by The River Wey Trust
Covers the Southern River Wey from its source near Haslemere
through to Tilford where it joins the northern branch. Gives
fascinating details on geology, industry, landscape and ecology of this
area. *ISBN 0-9514187-0-X reprinted Jan 1990, paperback, 46pp, well
illustrated*

John Owen Smith, publisher:—
www.johnowensmith.co.uk/books